QUEEN'S COLLEGE

The Senior Library, c. 1890.

QUEEN'S COLLEGE

150 Years and a New Century

Malcolm Billings

This book is dedicated to the thousands of young women who look back to their time at Queen's with great affection – especially my daughter Henrietta.

MALCOM BILLINGS
July 2000

ACKNOWLEDGEMENTS

The writing of this book has relied greatly on advice from many people in the College. A chance remark from a member of staff in the corridor for example often resulted in a fruitful line of enquiry. Many members of staff and old girls have proffered such leads which I have followed.

I am particularly grateful to Lady Goodhart and Jim Hutchinson for their guidance and patience in helping to piece together the disparate parts of the story for Queen's. Margaret Poulter, who catalogued the archives, bought forth dusty treasures that have enriched the historical facts. I pay great tribute to Dr Elaine Kaye for her painstaking research in the archives and for her helpful interest in the writing of this book.

It is no accident that a former Principal, Stephanie Fierz, is quoted many times. Hers has been a unique experience at Queen's, as student, teacher and Principal spanning more than 60 years. Her memories have been invaluable and constitute an archive in themselves. I am also grateful to another former Principal, Patricia Fleming, who kindly agreed to add her view of the College to my story. Other people who contributed to the production of this book include Jenny Fitz Gerald (Queen's College Librarian); Janice Lavery (Sesquicentennial Secretary); former students Lady Henderson, Diana Barnato Walker, Carole Bernard, Joan Healey, Susan Selwyn, Cindy Polemis, Michele Wade, Emma Wass and Karen (Kookie) Chammas.   MB

First published 2000
© Queen's College 2000
ISBN 0 907383 823

New photography by
John Spragg
Archival photography by
Godfrey New
Designed by Monica Matthews
and Eleanor Hayes

Printed in Great Britain by
Butler & Tanner Ltd

Published by
James & James (Publishers) Ltd
Gordon House Business Centre
6 Lissenden Gardens
London NW5 1LX

CONTENTS

FOREWORD

I have been associated with Queen's College for most of my thinking (and some of my unthinking) years. If I am judged to have succeeded, Queen's must accept some responsibility for this.

I first touched Queen's College in the early years of the war, around 1940, when I, like thousands of other children, was sent out of London – the war zone – to 'board' at the evacuated Queen's in Brackley, Oxfordshire. Memories of this time are vague except for a tall head girl, Janet Goddard, daughter of Theo Goddard, distinguished solicitor to Wallis Simpson; an even larger Headmistress, Miss Holloway, who sailed into Prayers like a battleship to port; and some bossy prefects. I was not happy, too young for the school and soon dispatched to distant North Wales to a boys' preparatory school ordered away from Frinton because of anticipated invasion – such wonderful years in Portmeirion. When the flying bombs were diving into London, Queen's bravely returned in 1944 to its London home in Harley Street. Then at Queen's there were few pupils but my intelligent news-reporting mother decided it was time for me to have a conventional education and to concentrate less on bad language and uneven learning – not to speak of discarding the rough grey shorts! I was accepted but surprised that on the first day I was shut in a small room to complete examination papers. Presumably I passed since I stayed without any obvious competition. I was later to learn of Miss Kynaston's concerns about me since she announced at the Staff meeting that 'we are going to have trouble with this one – she has been to a boys' preparatory school'. This heralded the start of some difficulties between us throughout the next few years.

Queen's after the war was faced with many problems – its own and the country's. Interesting girls came to the school, expansion occurred and it returned to its established ethos and success, providing high-standard teaching, not only of the three Rs but also of languages, science, domestic science and arts – all to include a mandatory weekly period in 'civics and constitution' – and it focused our preparation in the seniors for entry to university and the professions. We were encouraged to work hard, taught how to learn, keep our minds open, be tolerant of creed and other countries' customs, the weak and strong, and to be proud of being women. Whatever our aims – domestic, professional, explorer, artist – 'do it properly'. This was a school where gender differences were never highlighted and neither prizes nor class places were awarded.

The school flourished under the supervision of the steel blue eyes and chiselled features of Miss Kynaston, who gave her particular approval to those who were orderly, good at English and admired eighteenth-century English writers. I had none of these talents and awful writing. Still, Queen's did me proud, with outstanding physics teaching from Mrs Ethel Truman – a little legend who could make an idiot understand maths and me able to pass A-level physics with distinction. There was Miss Lambert, the biology teacher in the laboratory up the stairs from the Pfeiffer Hall, making botany and zoology exciting living subjects. From the four main subjects taken in Senior Science for Higher School Certificate (A-levels of today) I obtained exemption from first year MB for medicine. It was uncommon for girls' schools to provide this opportunity since physics and chemistry teaching rarely met the standards needed to compete for admission to medical school. I was accepted at Guy's Hospital in 2nd MB year, full of good lessons for life and a drive to get to the 'top' – wherever that was and despite anyone who said it was not possible.

Queen's years were happy, free, uniformless (except for the blazer), and stimulating. I made a few friends who I still see and love. I am pleased to see myself in the crowd photographed outside the school waving goodbye to HM The Queen Mother in 1948 – the occasion of the centenary – a day to remember. Who would have thought (certainly not I) that one day I would be Chairman of Council and perhaps, who knows, escort a Queen for Queen's College ?

One day, when I was training to be a Cardiologist in the National Heart Hospital in Westmoreland Street, Stephanie Fierz, the next Principal, who had briefly taught me science, asked me to become a Governor as she felt some youth was needed on the Council. I was thrilled as I admired the school greatly and knew I owed much to it. I have always felt fortunate that my mother had provided me with such a good education even if it did not include lessons in prudence, as my husband has often commented. I was happy that our daughter Kate went to Queen's and regretted that she left to go to boarding school.

I have served on the Council for thirty years with many chairmen, learnt much about the difficulties faced by independent schools and felt how foolish the Government was to stop the assisted places. It is so important to have good pupils from different backgrounds. I have not yet interfered much over these years except an occasional insistence that the Council adhered to the principles on which Queen's College was founded in 1848 – to provide higher (the highest) education for girls and if there were two possible paths, always take the most educationally élite.

This is a foreword to an interesting book which should bring happy memories to many. It shows the important part Queen's College has played in the education of women since its foundation in 1848. A new millennium, a new Chairman, a new Principal will bring changes, keeping up with the needs, demands and difficulties of the times and with new technology. Queen's will go forward, as always, expanding yet continuing to provide the best education for girls, looking after the individual so that each can take her rightful place in any society she chooses, being open-minded, able to learn, contribute and be secure in her knowledge. These are years not to be wasted. This is a book which tells you more than history.

Jane Somerville
Chairman of Governors
Summer 2000

CHAPTER ONE
'A GAGGLE OF GIRLS'

One word of warning . . . stairs.

THAT WAS A SIXTH-FORMER'S OPINION expressed in *The Other Prospectus* – a publication which Queen's College allows the girls in the Senior College to publish from time to time alongside the School's official prospectus.

For some the stairs are a severe form of institutional torture but for others:

'they do wonders for your thighs . . . they make up my main form of exercise'.

The staircases are a feature of Queen's. There are two superbly elegant ones in white stone with ornate cast-iron balustrades, and they are among the most impressive features of the building about which visitors always comment. Other staircases abound, as every teacher and pupil knows, but it is only the sheer number of them that makes it possible to move around, and through, the four large terrace houses and the buildings densely squeezed in behind them that comprise the College buildings in Harley Street in the West End of London. Queen's College was opened on this site in 1848 and has been there ever since.

43–49 Harley Street is an imposing sight; four tall houses – three of

them from the mid-eighteenth century with black-painted classical Georgian façades; the stucco outlined in brilliant white, with a projecting portico outside number 43.

The doorway to number 45 has been blocked off, and the fourth one, perched uncomfortably at the end of the row, number 49, is called Kynaston House after a post-war Principal. It is a distinguished Art Nouveau building with a red-brick façade, and was added to the end of the block at the turn of the last century. About 380 girls use the entrance at 49 where a general office by the front door keeps an eye on their comings and goings.

Inside the College you are met by a maze of rooms, corridors, and, of course, staircases. No one on the teaching staff has ever had time to count all the rooms but the surveyor's drawings show over 100 and about thirty staircases, which makes the architect's plan look like an oversized game of snakes and ladders. Two of the houses are known in architectural circles for their spacious atriums – features that have survived from the eighteenth century and which are now listed by English Heritage as rare in Harley Street, and therefore important to London's architectural heritage.

The top of the Georgian houses must be an equivalent climb to the fifth floor of a modern building, and, number 49, with its lower ceilings, is exactly that – a five-storey building.

The spaces have changed dramatically over the years. Sledgehammers have moved walls; plaster mouldings on ceilings suddenly stop where new smaller rooms have been created out of eighteenth-century spaciousness; bedrooms have become classrooms and offices; the wine cellar in the basement now contains musical instruments. Two carefully designed glass roofs were positioned down in the depths of the building to open up old light wells and have created an extension to the dining room, and a brightly painted junior common room has replaced a gloomy area of lockers.

The building changes all the time; builders arrive at the beginning of the summer holidays and have to be chased out just before the first day of term. During such a maintenance period in the early 1990s the girls arrived back to discover that the School's main thoroughfare, a wide long corridor that had been hollowed out of the ground floor of number 43 in the late nineteenth century, was almost unrecognizable. It had been refurbished in a richly coloured wallpaper of which William Morris would have been proud – a yellow and green floral motif chosen by the Principal, Lady Goodhart.

With indirect lighting to reflect off the vaults of the ceiling this décor must be unique among the capital's highly competitive day schools. 'Totally unsuitable for a school,' muttered some of the senior staff, but after several years there is hardly a mark on it, and both girls and staff are now rather proud of their floral main corridor.

In what was once the back garden of number 45 there is probably the smallest playground in London. It is not much more than a light well, a tiny square covered with imitation grass. The plastic grass is 'a bit naff', according to some of the girls, but they use two netball goals for practice anyway.

For games periods the junior girls join 'the crocodile' up Harley Street to Regent's Park where most of the games are played, but in the College senior girls claim some discretion: 'If you are sporty it is possible to play netball, hockey and rounders in the winter and tennis in the summer. If not, you do not have to do anything.'

There is, however, a gym that was added to the site when more of the mews at the back was taken over by Queen's, and where several champion fencers have been nurtured.

During the past 150 years architects have successfully squeezed in, and added on, new science laboratories, two language laboratories (visitors are sometimes surprised at what the girls sometimes manage to find via the satellite dish from Italian TV in the middle of the day), two IT laboratories, and a theatre studies workshop.

The place bursts into life soon after half past eight in the morning. Registration in the classrooms is at 8.40, and a hymn, a reading and a prayer, led by the Principal, Margaret Connell, the Deputy Principal, James Hutchinson, or the Head of English, Dr Eleanor Relle, start in the school hall at 8.50. Important announcements follow: a new system of swipe cards for paying in the self-service dining room; the departure of a school delegation to a UNESCO meeting in Paris; the new date for a field trip to the Orkney Islands; the news that Queen's has once again won the inter-school Latin play-reading competition; a reminder that the school parliament is about to meet; and a warning about lost property that has been lying around for two terms.

'Queen's is relaxed – not many rules but you can't abuse your freedom. None of the usual rules such as clothes, make-up, jewellery, etc.' The younger ones turn up in a sort of uniform anyway: jeans; T-shirts from their latest holiday or pop concert; baseball caps; sneakers or 'Doc

Facing page: A view of Harley Street today showing part of the College façade including the distinctive portico. Three of the buildings date from the late eighteenth century.

The College's main corridor is richly decorated with a floral-patterned wallpaper. The bust of a famous Old Girl, Gertrude Bell, looks on.

Martens' amazingly clumpy heavy-duty shoes. The seniors usually go through a phase of shorter and shorter skirts.

Most of the alterations have been reasonably sympathetic to the buildings' architectural history. The greatest loss, however, was the nineteenth-century science laboratory, which until the early 1980s had retained all its period features in a custom-built room with a skylight and in-built butlers' porcelain sinks and Bunsen burners with brass taps. As it was it could hardly have been used to teach modern science – it would have to have been left as a museum – but members of the staff who remember its demolition, and its transformation into two rooms, still sigh about its loss, and wish that an alternative had been possible. The lower part of the old laboratory is now full of rows of computers – Queen's was the first girls' school in the country to introduce computer studies.

The 'Waiting Room' – the first room on the right as you come into the main corridor – has not changed much in a century of music-making, meetings, lessons, and formal functions, and it has always been considered the heart of the School.

Some of the many facilities in use by pupils today include science (above) *and language laboratories* (below).

The carved door cases and mantelpieces were added in the early twentieth century, but the plasterwork on the ceiling – a swirling design with an angel in flight as its centrepiece – is believed by some historians to be an Adam design unchanged since the house was built in 1761. It inspired the muse in one girl who was there in the 1890s:

I remember, I remember
When my sums would not come right,
What consolation infinite
I've gained, and what delight
Where a plaster Cupid tries
To catch a little plaster bird
High in the plaster skies!

The Principal's office on the first floor of number 43 is another elegant room and throughout the buildings there are items of nineteenth-century furniture, some of which go back to the foundation of the School. The Senior College library is one example. It has made one move from the ground floor to the first floor, but in appearance it has not changed in a century or more; many of the mahogany bookcases are original and photographs taken at the turn of the century show the portraits on the walls and the furniture that the girls use today. It is certainly the most elegant and impressive room in the College which pupils remember with great affection years after their schooldays. One of the first impressions visitors get of Queen's is the informal atmosphere of girls curled up in big round cushions on the junior library floor; of teachers corralled in a corner by two or three pupils engaged in lively and uninhibited conversation.

The Principal is often confronted by puzzled parents who do not know what to call Queen's. Is it a college or a school? It is both, and while there is a distinction, everyone uses both terms interchangeably. The two names go back to its origins in the mid-nineteenth century. F. D. Maurice, the founder, called Queen's a college because his aim was to create higher education for women. But it was soon realized that a preparatory class was essential, and in 1849 the stables at the back were converted into what came to be known as 'Queen's College School'. The School today takes girls from 11 to 13 years; the Junior College is for 14–15-year-olds (usually with twenty to a class) while the Senior College consists of pupils in the A-level years. At the time of writing the 'sixth form' has over 100 pupils in tutor groups of about ten.

It is not possible for a girl to go to Queen's without being affected by the echoes of the past. To the delight of many pupils, they are sometimes taken out into Harley Street to consider the School buildings in the context of a grand urban design first mooted by John Holles, Duke of Newcastle. He bought the Marylebone Estate in 1708, and, according to Nikolaus Pevsner's *Buildings of England* laid out Cavendish Square and its surrounding grid of streets.

All the streets are family names: the Duke's daughter Henrietta, married Edward Harley, the Earl of Oxford and Mortimer. Their daughter, Lady Margaret Cavendish Harley married William Bentinck, the second Duke of Portland. All these names can be seen on the street signs. The estate remained in the hands of the Portland family until 1870 when it passed to Lord Howard de Walden.

Harley Street itself was started about 1729, but the recession of 1731 brought the development scheme to a halt, including the centrepiece of the plan, a palatial town house in Cavendish Square.

Only two buildings from the eighteenth century survive in the Square: a pair of stone-faced Palladian houses built about 1770. However, the church of St Peter, Vere Street, built as a chapel for the new estate in 1721, and where F. D. Maurice preached in his later years,

Theatre studies. Many girls have gone on to make a career in the theatre.

Harley Street, c.1880. As well as doctors, the street has had many famous residents including the Duke of Wellington, Gladstone and Florence Nightingale.

11

is a delightful little church with a fine portico, a Venetian window, and galleries that run around the interior on three sides. It was used by the College as its church for many years. The Marylebone Parish Church has also been used by Queen's but in the 1980s the College began to hold its services at the larger Nash church, All Souls in Langham Place, opposite Broadcasting House.

The first families to buy leases arrived in Harley Street in 1752. It was then, as now, an expensive upmarket place to live, and the list of distinguished residents included Horatio Nelson's widow; the Duke of Wellington; the Earl of Mulgrave (military adviser to the eighteenth-century Prime Minister William Pitt) and an assortment of admirals, dukes, and literary figures. The great Victorian Liberal Prime Minister, Gladstone, lived at number 73, and in number 43, one of the College buildings, lived Lord Strangford, the poet and politician whose main claim to fame was his reputation for having fought the last duel in England in 1852.

There is a blue plaque on one of the houses in Upper Harley Street recording the fact that Frederick Denison Maurice lived there from 1862 to 1866.

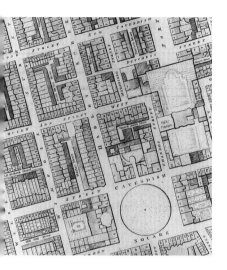

Harwoods map, 1792, shows Cavendish Square and the surrounding area. The Duke of Newcastle's grid-like design is clearly preserved.

Cavendish Square, from a reproduction of an aquatint by Thomas Malton, c.1800.

Florence Nightingale opened a hospital at number 90 Harley Street and according to Gordon Mackenzie's book *Marylebone,* the first Harley Street doctor practised in what is now one of the College buildings – number 47. His name was Dr William Rowley, 'an army surgeon from 1760 to 1765, settled down to general practice at number 66 Harley Street' (now 47, the street was renumbered in the nineteenth century). Describing himself as a 'man-midwife', he built up a very profitable connection and made a fortune.

Charles Dickens was very rude about the street when he described it in *Little Dorrit:*

St Peter's Church, Vere Street, where special services were held for the College and where F. D. Maurice preached.

> Like unexceptional Society, the opposing rows of houses in Harley Street were very grim with one another. Indeed, the mansions and their inhabitants were so much alike in that respect, that the people were often to be found drawn up on opposite sides of dinner-tables, in the shade of their own loftiness, staring at the other side of the way with the dullness of the houses.

Queen's, however, can look back on someone who sounds anything but dull – the portrait painter Allan Ramsay. He lived at number 45 and was appointed official portrait painter to George III. It is said that the house was a lively place and always full of the best painters and writers of the day. Ramsay converted the hayloft and coachman's house into a studio and long gallery, and when he started on a portrait of Queen Charlotte, he asked for the crown jewels and other items of royal regalia to be sent to Harley Street. Such was his reputation that the jewels arrived along with an armed guard who waited until Her Majesty's portrait was finished as well as fifty others which were destined for various palaces and government offices as a job lot.

Allan Ramsay. Self-portrait, 1776.

Most girls are aware of the history surrounding their school, but they also agree that: 'It's brilliant going to a school that has John Lewis's as the corner shop!'

Traditional female accomplishments in the nineteenth century included reading, embroidery and playing the piano.

CHAPTER TWO

A WOMAN'S PLACE

MOST WOMEN IN THE NINETEENTH CENTURY had very little control over their day-to-day life, let alone their destiny. Fathers, brothers and husbands laid down the guidelines and women were either happy to comply or were resigned to the inevitability of male supremacy. The problem of a woman achieving anything approaching equality is surely summed up in the following proposition:

> Seeing that the average brain weight of women is about five ounces less than that of men, on merely anatomical grounds we should be prepared to expect a marked inferiority of intellectual power in the former.

That conclusion was put forward in a lecture, 'Mental Differences between Men and Women', by an eminent Victorian scientist George J. Romanes. A graduate of Cambridge, and a friend of Charles Darwin, he wrote profusely about evolution. His interest in the size of the female cranium led him to utter this warning: 'the physique of young women as a class is not sufficiently robust to stand the strain of severe study'. He also noted that some girls who were being educated at high schools could indeed stand up to long hours, 'but that only goes to show of what good stuff our English girls are made'.

'Patronizing rubbish' would be the appropriate response from a Queen's girl today, but many in that Victorian audience would have nodded vigorously in agreement. What is even more shocking about that lecture is the date, 1887, when so many of the early important battles to educate women had been fought and won, including the introduction of academic education for women at Queen's College. George J. Romanes went on to concede in his lecture that education for women had taken root in 'modern' society, but he assured his listeners that the basic differences between men and women could not be ignored:

> We rarely find in women that firm tenacity of purpose and determination to overcome obstacles which is characteristic of what we call a manly mind. When a woman is urged to any prolonged or powerful exercise of volition, the prompting cause is usually to be found in the emotional side of her nature, whereas in man we may generally observe that the intellectual is alone sufficient to supply the needed motive . . . their minds are more prone to what is called 'wandering' and we seldom find that they have specialized their studies or pursuits to the same extent as is usual among men.

A cartoon by Sir John Tenniel in Punch, *1871, illustrates a wife's life of drudgery. 'I say, Joe, dear, if you can't enjoy your supper now you have lost your grumble about nine hours – grumble for me, as I've done fourteen, and ain't finished yet.'*

Despite the evidence to the contrary, male prejudice in the late nineteenth century had decreed that, while there were obvious benefits in education, too much of a good thing was in danger of wrecking the fabric of nineteenth-century English society.

The middle classes had a clear idea of the role that women should play. They should aspire to marry well, be good homemakers, and rear children. There was no question of women seeking a career, and, at the beginning of Queen Victoria's reign in 1837, there were of course no women doctors, lawyers, company directors, bankers, or even civil servants.

Middle-class women either married or stayed at home where they amused themselves with a social round of visits, philanthropic works, and seeing to the 'education' of their daughters.

Opportunities for what we would regard as a well-rounded education for women were almost non-existent, and, even if the required standard were attained, the universities would not accept women as full-time students or give them a degree. They were also banned from the meetings of many learned societies. The Geological Society and the Ethnological Society, however, were two that would allow women to attend if the discussion were considered to be in a 'popular' vein.

While a young man of a family of means automatically went off to a public school to be prepared for a career in commerce, the professions, or in the colonies, early Victorian society took the view that higher education for a girl was not only a waste of time but was a positive bar to finding a husband. It was obvious to any mother who sought the best for her daughter that men did not want so-called 'bluestocking' wives who might embarrass them by discussing politics and economics and science instead of music, art, and flower-arranging. Such women, it was thought, had forfeited their femininity and would not make good wives.

Anyone in doubt could turn to authors such as Mrs Sarah Ellis who gave advice in the pages of *Women of England, Sons of the Soil,* and *Hints to make Home Happy.* In *Daughters of England* published in 1845 she advised:

So far as cleverness, learning and knowledge are conducive to woman's moral excellence, they are desirable, and no farther. All that would occupy her mind to the exclusion of better things, all that would involve her in the mazes of flattery and admiration, all that would tend to draw away her thoughts from others and fix them on herself, ought to be avoided as an evil to her.

Perhaps the worst aspect of life for the intelligent shrinking violet was her complete dependence on her husband. Once married, her money and land became the husband's property, and divorce was rarely possible.

The wealthy and upper classes usually educated their daughters at home with the help of governesses, and then at a limited number of expensive boarding schools where they might learn about deportment, geography, history, and sometimes science. But in the opinion of Frances Power Cobbe, the nineteenth-century feminist and writer who attended such a school, 'Nobody dreamed that any one of us could in later life be more, or less, than an ornament of society . . . everything was taught us in the inverse ratio of its true importance. At the bottom of the scale were morals and religion, and at the top were music and dancing.'

Such an educational experience could cost as much as £500 for a year – a fortune in the first part of the nineteenth century.

The cheaper boarding schools for the less wealthy would cost about £100 a year. Dorothea Beale, who was one of the first pupils to enrol at Queen's College when it opened in 1848, and who went on to become the renowned Principal of Cheltenham Ladies' College, and to found St Hilda's College, Oxford, recalled her own schoolgirl experience before she went to Queen's:

> Our mistresses were women who had read and thought; they had taken great pains to arrange various schemes of knowledge; yet what miserable teaching we had in many subjects; history was learned by committing to memory little manuals; rules of arithmetic were taught but the principles were never explained; we repeated week by week the Lamentations of King Hezekiah . . . and the worst doggerel verses on the solar system.

Above all, the girls were taught how to behave like ladies, and much time was spent practising the correct form for the wording of letters to people of varying social grades, and writing out invitations and acceptances. The teachers were often known as 'aunt' in an attempt to create a homely image for the institution. Girls from such schools usually left at 16 or 17 years of age, and in many cases went on to finishing schools abroad, which for Dorothea was a fashionable school for English girls in the Champs Elysées in Paris:

Frances Power Cobbe, 1822–1904, Irish social worker, feminist and prominent anti-vivisectionist. She was associated with Mary Carpenter in the founding of ragged schools and published more than thirty works, mostly on social issues.

Imagine our disgust at being required to read English History . . . to learn by heart all Murray's *Grammar*, to learn even lists of prepositions by heart. We used indeed to read collectively Robertson's *Charles the Fifth*, i.e. it was read aloud on dancing evenings. Each class went in succession for the dancing lesson; thus no one read the whole book, though the school in its corporate capacity did.

For young middle-class ladies from 10 to 14 years of age small day schools attempted to do the same job. They were establishments run by proprietors who could be relied upon not to transform girls in their care into 'bluestockings'. They learned by rote the dates of history and the rules of English grammar, dancing, needlework, and the piano.

But for the great bulk of the population there was a hotchpotch of charitable, church and so-called 'Dame Schools'. The latter were small local schools for working-class families that cost about fourpence a week and were run by 'teachers' who set up classes in their own front room.

The curriculum was simple, needlework and learning by rote, and in many of the schools children probably ended up with as much a grip on the three Rs as the young ladies at the expensive establishments.

Sketch of Cheltenham Ladies' College in 1873, and (inset) *its principal, Dorothea Beale, who was one of the first students at Queen's when it opened in 1848.*

19

Millicent Fawcett (1847–1929), suffragette, educational reformer, and founder of Newnham College, Cambridge (1871). She was the younger sister of Elizabeth Garrett Anderson, the medical pioneer who was a member of the Council of Queen's.

Charlotte Brontë (1816–55), whose stories about governesses drew attention to their plight.

Then there were free Sunday schools. Started with an evangelical purpose in the eighteenth century, they also taught boys and girls to read, and, in some Nonconformist churches, to write as well. Some Sunday schools put in a long day, starting at eight in the morning and finishing at four o'clock in the afternoon. But, as June Purvis in *A History of Women's Education in England* points out, for many working-class girls in the industrial towns it was all the education they would ever get.

Most working-class boys and girls, whose parents insisted on sending them to school, attended weekday schools run by the Church of England National Society and the smaller British and Foreign Society.

The societies had devised a system of teaching based on monitors, other older children who taught the younger ones. The monitors earned a few pence a week and the schools employed only one teacher who trained the monitors. Inevitably the quality of the teaching was abysmal because the monitors, hardly educated themselves and not much older that their pupils, were trained to teach by rote. They could spot when the children went wrong but that was all. With only a curtain down the middle of the room to separate the sexes it must have seemed like bedlam as the monitors rapped out the rhythm of the rote.

When these schools were set up in the early nineteenth century the main topic was scripture, but the curriculum broadened with time, and, by the middle of the century, the schools were also teaching writing and reading, ciphering (arithmetic), religious exercises, and saying prayers. If it was a mixed school, in the afternoon the girls would concentrate on needlework and knitting. June Purvis in her study of education and the working class, concluded: 'What becomes clear is that the proper station in life for working-class girls was considered to be a domestic situation, usually within the home, as a good servant and then as a wife and mother . . . the National and British schools carried the stigma of charity and were seen as an imposition upon working-class life, and provided by the middle classes.'

Some children were left out altogether, those who ran wild in big cities like London. The government-aided societies shut them out because of their filthy clothes and rowdy behaviour. In order to get them off the streets, the philanthropic Lord Shaftesbury started the 'ragged School Union', which by 1858 was educating over 100,000 children in 128 ragged schools, in London and the surrounding rural areas.

Although most women accepted the *status quo* in the nineteenth century there had been a long history of challenge to the concept of male superiority. The philosopher Mary Astell (1668–1731) wrote that women would have to take control of their own education if they were to gain equality, and that a women's university was the way to proceed.

She was probably the first to make such a radical suggestion in England. Other women who alarmed society with their views included Catherine Macaulay (1731–91) and a remarkable young woman called Mary Wollstonecraft. Born in 1759 she survived a peripatetic childhood dominated by a drunken spendthrift father.

What education she had picked up along the way was enough to get her a job as a governess. Very critical of the way the upper classes neglected their daughters' education she left the schoolroom and in 1788 came to London at the invitation of a publisher who had seen her pamphlet *Thoughts on the Education of Daughters*. In 1792 she rattled the male establishment, and encouraged the next generation of reformers who founded Queen's College, with her book inspired by revolutionary ideas in France, *Vindication of the Rights of Women*.

She accused men of denying women education and turning them into toys: 'Gentleness, docility, and spaniel-like affection are . . . consistently recommended as the cardinal virtues of the sex. She was created to be the toy of man, his rattle, and it must jingle in his ears whenever, dismissing reason, he chooses to be amused.'

Mary Wollstonecraft's opinion on late eighteenth-century boys' schools was equally trenchant, especially at 'speech day' when the boys were polished up to impress their parents: 'How much time is lost in teaching them to recite what they do not understand? Whilst seated on benches, all in their best array, the mamas listen with astonishment to the parrot-like prattle, uttered in solemn cadences, with all the pomp of ignorance and folly. Yet how can these things be reined whilst schoolmasters depend entirely on parents for a subsistence; and, when so many rival schools hang out their lures to catch the attention of vain fathers and mothers?'

Almost a century ahead of her time Mary Wollstonecraft proposed an education system that could solve the problem – a national network of day schools:

> To render this possible, day schools for particular ages should be established by the Government, in which boys and girls should be educated together. The school for the younger children, from 5 to 9

Mary Kingsley (1862–1900), niece of Charles Kingsley, one of the first professors of Queen's College. Although not formally educated, she was a voracious reader in her father's scientific library. Her work Travels in West Africa *was based on her diaries kept during her stay on the continent where she lived among and bartered with the natives while retaining European dress.*

years of age ought to be absolutely open to all classes . . . and to prevent any of the distinctions of vanity they should all be dressed alike . . . botany, mechanics, and astronomy; reading writing and arithmetic, natural history, and some simple experiments in natural philosophy might fill up the day but these pursuits should never encroach on gymnastic play in the open air. Elements of religion, the history of man and politics, might also be taught by conversations in Socratic form.

The self-educated Mary went on to suggest that after primary education those less academically inclined, and therefore destined for domestic employment and the mechanical trades, should continue in a co-educational school that taught such skills. Those ideas, which attracted such epithets as 'hyena in petticoats', were widely published in Britain and on the Continent and were an inspiration to those families who encouraged their daughters to become more than just social butterflies and good wives.

Some girls from middle-class backgrounds did manage to educate themselves, often despite their parents, and go on to lead an intellectual life. Mary Somerville (1780–1872), at the age of 10, was sent to a boarding school to learn to read. She said in her autobiography that the School was typical of the late eighteenth century where deportment was considered so important that she had to wear an iron collar to keep her head up as she walked around the School. Back at home Mary read all the books she could lay her hands on and by the time she was 14 was reading Euclid and books about algebra:

> I had to take part in household affairs, and to make and mend my own clothes. I rose early, played on the piano and painted during the time I could spare in the daylight hours, but I sat up very late reading Euclid. The servants, however, told my mother 'It is no wonder the stock of candles is soon exhausted, for Miss Mary sits up reading till a very late hour' whereupon an order was given to take away the candle as soon as I was in bed.

At first light, wrapped in a blanket, she began reading again by the window until the daily chores of sewing and housework began. Marriage did not stop her from reading although her first husband, an army officer, resented her interest in learning. He died young and in 1812 Mary

Mary Wollstonecraft (1759–97), feminist and writer of the controversial Vindication of the Rights of Woman *which advocated equality of the sexes and equal opportunities in education. She married the political writer and novelist William Godwin and gave birth to a daughter, Mary, later to become Mary Shelley, author of* Frankenstein.

married William Somerville who encouraged his wife to study and write her most famous book *The Mechanism of the Heavens*, published in 1827. More remarkable books followed as did international recognition for her work as a scientist. Somerville College, Oxford, was named after her.

Other women who broke through the barriers of male chauvinism included Florence Nightingale, the gifted mathematician Ada Lovelace (the daughter of the poet Byron), and the writers Elizabeth Sewell, Charlotte M. Yonge, Jane Austen, and the Brontë sisters.

But girls from families in which there was a tradition of learning had a much easier time. The sisters of F. D. Maurice (founder of Queen's College), for example, grew up in a household in which education for women was not an issue; their father, Michael, was a Nonconformist clergyman who also ran his own school and from an early age the children assisted their father in the schoolroom.

The eldest daughter, Mary Maurice, started her own school and went on to play an important national role in the development of women's education. She wrote several books on the subject and was one of the early supporters of the Governesses' Benevolent Institution. Indeed the 'plight' of the English governess was the catalyst that led to the opening of Queen's College, Harley Street.

Mary Somerville, Scottish scientific writer and author of The Mechanism of the Heavens *and several other works. She gave her name to Somerville College, Oxford.*

An idealized portrayal of the governess's role – the reality was often very different.

CHAPTER THREE

A GENTEEL OCCUPATION

They were worse paid than the cook; their salaries would bear poor comparison with the wages of the butler; they would appear but shabbily with the remuneration of the lady's maid.

CHARLES DICKENS WAS CHEERED when he made those comments in a speech to the Governesses' Benevolent Institution in 1844. The 32-year-old novelist and social campaigner had taken an interest in the 'plight' of the English governess, and, for several years, gave his support to the institution. On the occasion of that speech, in front of an audience of monied and titled well-wishers, he warmed to his theme of society's disregard of 'knowledge' while getting in a dig at the current fashion in head scarves.

The power of governesses was acknowledged by the middle-aged lady in a turban – she felt the power of the governess's knowledge in the education of her daughters; gentlemen also felt the power of the governess's knowledge; but nobody thought of the poor fagged knowledge herself, her eyes red with poring over advertisements in search of a new situation; and having faithfully accomplished her task in one family, being thrown upon the world.

Dickens had summed up the problems for these women in a few lines. Governesses were in great demand in Dickensian England, and

Some governesses abroad preferred the relative independence of starting a small school of their own. A group from Miss England's High School for Girls on a picnic at Dixon's Creek, Queensland, Australia.

throughout the nineteenth century the English governess spread her influence across the world from Moscow to Capetown and from New York to Bangkok. They popped up among the offspring of the ruling classes everywhere. In Vienna Miss May became governess to the Archduchess Elizabeth Marie, granddaughter of the Emperor of Russia. The Governesses' Benevolent Institution says that, 'she knew nothing of court etiquette, but such was her demeanour, everyone said "You are so natural."' What more could an Emperor ask.

Anna Leonowens became famous for writing about her time as an English governess at the Siamese Court. Miss Emmeline Lott also wrote her memories of teaching the only son of Ismael Pasha, the Viceroy of Egypt. Maria Graham was hired by the Brazilian Court to be Brazil's first and only Imperial governess, and all over Europe, according to Governesses' Benevolent Institution records 'governesses lived on to a ripe old age in the draughty, ancient castles belonging to the mid-European aristocracy. More often than not they were buried in the huge stone vaults of the family with whom they had become completely identified.'

Less than twenty years after Charles Dickens's eloquent support for the Governesses' Benevolent Institution an attempt to promote the mass export of governesses began. The Female Middle Class Emigration Society was set up in 1862 to assist young governesses to work in the colonies in India, North America, Africa, and Australasia. Most of the candidates chose Australia and New Zealand.

The founder of the society, Maria Rye, not only wanted opportunities for English women to work but also to make a contribution to the moral values in the English-speaking parts of the Empire: 'and if the vice and immorality on either side of the Atlantic is ever to be uprooted, it must be by some further extension of emigration, by the steady departure from these shores of our superfluous workers, and by an influx into the colonies of a body of women infinitely superior by birth, by education, and by taste, to the hordes of wild uneducated creatures we have hitherto sent abroad'. The Governesses' Benevolent Institution was slow to get involved but by 1879 the Committee was talking about the possibility of helping governesses in London to start a new life in the colonies. The Institution's records show, 'a number of women were assisted to go to Australia. Four years later an inquiry was received as to the working of the Institution from the Governesses' Institute and Melbourne Home.'

The Female Middle Class Emigration Society's target was at least 150,000 English governesses, but the girls wrote back about horrific three-month voyages to Melbourne and Sydney travelling second class, and about Australians not appreciating the finer points of a governess's role. 'Australian children are just like the vegetation here for neither appear to submit to much control. Pineapples, peaches, and the finest fruit grow in the open air without care and the children are equally wild and impetuous.' Such comments, reprinted in Patricia Clark's study of *The Governesses – Letters from the Colonies, 1862–1882,* were sent back to the Female Middle Class Emigration Society in London along with repayments for the loans they were given to get them to the Antipodes. Others wrote back saying that there was no point in sending girls who were not well qualified. 'They would be better off at home,' one of them wrote. The ability to teach music was paramount, and not all governesses could do it. In the cities jobs were hard to get; so many decided to open their own schools instead, and one governess in Melbourne resorted to playing the piano and singing in a hotel.

Others wrote glowing letters about colonial life, about the wonders of the bush and the climate and the kindness they had received from people on sheep stations where the main conversation was about – sheep. But one governess warned, 'You meet with as much cool hauteur in a Melbourne drawing room as you ever would in an English one.' The governess with the teaching job from hell must have been Ellen Ollard who answered an advertisement for a job in the country, north of Melbourne. 'It was supposed to be as companion to a young lady, but when I arrived there I found that there was no servant kept and the man was a travelling hawker and I was supposed to help his daughter make fancy articles for sale and do all the housework besides, so I did not stay very long.'

The ideals of the Society were never fully realized. A governess's Eldorado in the goldfields of New South Wales and Victoria failed to materialize and only about 300 women took part over the twenty-year period of the scheme. However, the majority of the governesses who went out did not come back, having blended into colonial society realizing that conditions at home might be even tougher.

By the middle of the century the demand for governesses at home had grown substantially. The idea of a governess appealed to the burgeoning number of families in the social spectrum who were upwardly mobile, as a way of educating a clutch of children cheaply, in the secure environment of the home.

Merchants, millowners, and manufacturers with newly acquired wealth could also ape their social betters by adding a governess to their indoor staff.

A governess could come in several different guises: nursery governess, daily governess, or visiting governess. The most usual arrangement tied the governess to the family for seven days a week, in a job that might last ten or fifteen years until the last daughter went off to boarding school. The plum jobs were often with wealthy old-established families who would have employed a substantial indoor staff: a butler, footmen, maids, children's nurse, and perhaps two governesses – one in the nursery and another to deal with the older children. A governess with such families could have been sure of a room to herself – perhaps a sitting room as well, and a schoolroom in which to work. She would eat with the family, go to church with them, and accompany the young ladies on outings with perhaps a footman in attendance. The schoolroom routine might also have been broken by the arrival of visiting masters who taught music, dancing, and foreign languages.

At the other end of the scale the governess might have had to share a room with some of her charges and be expected to help with all the daily chores. Status would certainly have been in doubt, but in some ways that job might have been less lonely.

In the big houses governesses often complained that, while to all intents and purposes they were members of the family, they were expected to keep their distance. Governesses often agonized as to whether or not to spend the evening in the drawing room with the family. But social events could be even more difficult. Anne Brontë put these words into the mouth of her fictional governess Agnes Grey who described what it was like walking to church with her pupils and her friends.

> It was disagreeable to walk beside them, as if listening to what they said, or wishing to be thought one of them, while they talked over me or across, and if their eyes, in speaking, chanced to fall on me it seemed as if they looked on vacancy – as if they neither did not see me or were very desirous to make it appear so.

A particularly humiliating stage for the governess was during her pupils' adolescence when the governess had to take them through the intricate rules of etiquette concerning young men and courtship. Charlotte Brontë, the most famous of the literary sisters, wrote from personal experience as a governess, and had a connection with Queen's College. The letters, written to her publishers in London shortly after she had written *Jane Eyre* refer to a Queen's student, Mary Louisa Williams. She was the daughter of the publisher's reader William Smith Williams. Charlotte Brontë visited the Williams family in London and on 3 July 1849 wrote to say that she was glad that Louisa had a chance of presentation to Queen's College: 'I hope that she will succeed. Come what may afterwards, an education received is an advantage gained – a priceless advantage.' By 26 July 1849 Louisa had indeed enrolled at Queen's and her certificates of qualification are still in the archives. No evidence has yet emerged to show that any of the Brontë sisters visited Queen's, but Charlotte, who was a great admirer of F. D. Maurice, clearly knew all about the College and approved of what it stood for.

Kathryn Hughes in her book *The Victorian Governess* explains how the governess had to double as a sexual policewoman, making sure that her teenage pupils never went anywhere without a chaperone:

> It was part of . . . curiously confused thinking about young women that they were believed to be both sexually unawakened and inviolable, yet constantly in danger of being corrupted by contact with men . . . single women up to the age of thirty and frequently beyond were chaperoned wherever they went by their mother or another married woman. Any girl who broke this code by walking in public alone forfeited the sexual good name which was integral to being a lady. What made the contradiction in the governess's situation so humiliatingly apparent was the fact that in similar circumstances she was not considered to need a companion: the implication was not that she had no honour, simply that it was inconceivable that anyone should wish to deprive her of it.

Some governesses were natural carers and educators, but the diaries of many of those who decided to take on the job leave the impression that they had no other choice of work. In the volatile market-place of Victorian England family businesses collapsed leaving debt instead of income, fathers died prematurely, and elder brothers or cousins either could not, or would not, pick up the tab for unmarried relatives. Moreover, there were many more females than males in Victorian England, so spinsters left on the shelf were a statistical inevitability. The

An apprehensive child is urged to shake hands with her new governess (1892).

census of England and Wales in 1851 showed an imbalance of about half a million. Large numbers of women had to fend for themselves, despite advice from all sides, which cautioned a young woman against paid work if she wished to retain her status as a lady.

To square this social circle the Victorians agreed that being a governess was perfectly respectable. As she lived with a family and taught the children, she would be under the protection of her employer, who, it was argued, would simply carry through the governess's father's responsibility to ensure her security and good reputation. The money was purely incidental.

But in a crowded market-place where supply exceeded demand, employers could choose from the output of training schools that specialized in grooming daughters of the clergy to be governesses. Charlotte Brontë drew on her own experience as a governess when she described one of those establishments in *Jane Eyre*. But for the most part the governesses would go to their employers equipped with the same faulty education as the ladies who hired them.

Dorothea Beale's mother was an exception. She had been brought up in an educated household, and was more than capable of assessing the quality of a new governess. Dorothea described the problem her mother had had in the early 1840s of finding someone who could spell.

Hundreds of replies came in from just one advertisement. The initial sifting eliminated the poor spellers; 'next the wording and composition were criticised, and lastly a few of the writers were interviewed and a selection was made. But alas! an inspection of our exercise books revealed so many uncorrected faults that dismissal followed, and another search resulted in the same way.'

As Charles Dickens made plain in his speech to the worthies of the GBI, pay was a big problem. The market was overcrowded (as Mrs Beale discovered) and employers were quick to take advantage of their position. Pay ranged from £20 to £100 per annum. But, in desperation, some pretended they had private means and would waive the salary just to get a roof over their heads. The satirical magazine *Punch* wrote its version of a governess's reply to an advertisement for a job.

> If I have any emotion in excess, it is that of the love of children; a quality, perhaps, only second to that of plain and ornamental needlework. My activity never permits me to have a moment's leisure; and my good temper, from the time of infancy, has passed into family proverb. You

'A housemaid interrupts a lesson to deliver a message. While the governess's dress and deportment announce her to be a lady, the housemaid's sulky deference suggests that the status of the governess, as far as the servants are concerned, is open to challenge.' (K. Hughes, The Victorian Governess, *1882).*

30

state, Sir, and I admire your frankness – that no salary will be given. I fully understand, Sir, that the delightful privilege of dwelling under your roof, and enjoying the pure moral atmosphere of your hearth, must exceed any value to be awarded by the coined dross of this selfish world. How happy am I that, possessing a sufficient competence of my own, I may give myself up heart, and soul, and pocket, to the formation of the minds of your children, and to the daily execution of your needlework . . .

P.S. Pray do not pay the postage of your letter. I shall esteem it as a touching earnest of your friendship, if you will allow me to pay the twopence.

Most governesses, however, were paid – even if not quite enough to keep a wardrobe fashionable and in good condition.

There were other problems that social campaigners with an interest in governesses tried to address. Mary Maurice drew attention in her book *Governess Life*, published in 1849, to the fact that no contracts or letters of agreement were exchanged between governess and employer.

> For want of such a document, many a poor governess, through the versatility or want of consideration of her employers, has been thrown out of a good situation; whilst they had no power to claim their rights; and families have been inconvenienced in like manner by the misconduct of their teachers. Cases are not infrequent in which the latter had adopted the dishonourable plan of engaging herself to a situation she preferred, before she had expressed any wish to quit.

The whole business of hiring and firing was a nightmare for governesses, and survival between jobs without sufficient capital to tide them over was a major problem that for some was resolved in the workhouse.

This state of affairs had been recognized as early as 1829 when the Governesses' Mutual Assurance Society was set up to help members who had become sick or unemployed. It petered out after several years and a new start was made in 1841. Again it languished for lack of support until two years later when the Revd David Laing agreed to become its Honorary Secretary. Renamed the Governesses' Benevolent Institution, it redefined its objectives as being 'to raise the character of governesses as a class and thus improve the tone of female education;

'They were worse paid than the cook; their salaries would bear poor comparison with the wages of the butler.'
Charles Dickens, 1844.

to assist governesses in making provision for their old age and those governesses whose exertions for their parents or families have prevented such a provision'.

The need was great and increasing year by year. In 1861 the census figures showed that one-fifth of the governesses in employment at that time were over 40 years of age. That was a sizeable proportion of the 25,000 who put down their profession as governess. The census also revealed that several dozen governesses were still working at the age of 80.

The Victorian age also produced a remarkable parson, David Laing. According to the records of the GBI, he first worked in London as chaplain of the Middlesex Hospital, and Hon. Chaplain of the St Ann's Society Schools: 'A man of the highest integrity and intellect, he was hardworking, conscientious and above all, human.' While running the GBI he also re-established the Anglican Church of Holy Trinity in St Pancras, North London. He carried the full responsibility for the building of the church guaranteeing the full amount of £3,000 through insurance on his life.

Laing had good contacts in educational circles. He won the support of women such as Mary Maurice and Frances Mary Buss, who went on to found the North London Collegiate School in 1850 with Laing as one of the patrons. Elaine Kaye, in her comprehensive history of the College, found that the Honourable Amelia Murray, Maid of Honour to Queen Victoria, was an important influence in Laing's endeavour and contributed generously. 'During a long life she supported many philanthropic schemes; she was also a person of some spirit, for in 1856 she resigned her position in the Queen's bedchamber after a visit to the United States, so that she could be free to advocate the abolition of slavery.' It is assumed that her influence was instrumental in securing Queen Victoria's support of the Institution and later of Queen's College. It is of interest that in 1847 Amelia Murray published a book entitled *Remarks on Education*, in which she expressed ideas which had much in common with those of Maurice, disapproving of corporal punishment in any school, and the element of competition between pupils. The scene was set for a new sort of school as David Laing, with his social connections, put together a committee of wealthy and motivated patrons and raised enough money to take a lease on what is now 47 Harley Street in 1845.

The house became the first Home for governesses who could stay there between jobs. During the first six months fifty-two governesses were

Revd David Laing, Secretary of the Governesses' Benevolent Institution who created the Home for governesses in Harley Street and set up the first courses for the education of governesses.

Frederick Denison Maurice. The painting by Lowes Dickenson hangs in the Senior Library.

The Revd Charles Kingsley. The painting which hangs in the Kynaston Library is by A. Edmund Dyer after Lowes Dickenson.

The Royal Charter (above) *and Royal Seal* (below) *which was attached to the document.*

The Home for governesses at 47 Harley Street. Queen's College began in the house next door to it.

offered board and lodgings at a rate they could afford.

The Harley Street house, however, had another function – as an employment agency. Changing jobs was often traumatic, involving expensive advertisements, agency fees, endless correspondence (from a 'respectable' address), and weeks or months of waiting around. The register outlining the needs and aspirations of both parties was an immediate success. Registration was free and of the 694 governesses who had put their names down by the end of 1846, 343 had found employment two years later. The numbers grew every year as did the success of the provident fund. It gave governesses the opportunity to pay in a small part of their salary to buy an annuity for their retirement. Funds were also raised to distribute to governesses who had fallen on hard times.

One year after the opening of the Home a reporter from Chambers' *Edinburgh Journal* visited Harley Street and wrote his impressions.

'The door was opened by a respectable servant in livery.' So far so good. The reporter had already noted that it was a 'good house in a good Street'. He was then shown into the registration office where he was again impressed by the 'inmate' in charge of the building.

I soon discovered that she was an educated person, clever, active, and experienced in managing a large establishment; besides having a heart full of sympathy for those who are placed around her. After seeing the registration books and talking over their usefulness, the housekeeper ... took me across an inner hall to a handsome dining room. I observed there two harps and a piano or two. These had been presented to the home by some friends of the Institution ... This room, with its bay window, looked remarkably cheerful in the bright sunlight: so free from noise or disquietude, it seemed to me that it must be a perfect Elysium to those who come here to rest a while from the worry of the schoolroom.

When the reporter visited the Home there was accommodation for twenty-five governesses, most of whom had to share the big rooms by curtaining off sections for themselves. There were rooms with two beds and some single rooms.

In one of the upper rooms there was an invalid – a girl of 17 – for whom the housekeeper told me every one in the house was interested. She could not rise from the bed, and the other inmates vied with each other in attention to her. One lady was reading when the housekeeper knocked on the door to inquire how the patient then was. She came out to speak to us, and I was charmed to see the strong interest which she felt for her young charge whose illness is, alas, consumption.

A Home for elderly governesses was opened in Kentish Town in North London in 1849.

Although not included in the original objectives of the Institution, David Laing was keenly interested in providing education for governesses, along with certificates of competence. As early as 1844 he began taking soundings among Church educationalists and at the government Education Department, and, by the spring of 1847, had gathered around him a group of academics from King's College London who had agreed to give lectures at the Home. Royal approval for the name of the College was quickly acquired and a substantial donation promised by the Queen who also agreed to be the patron of the College. In the same year the Poet Laureate Alfred Tennyson published a long poem in blank verse called 'The Princess'. It was about a college presided over by the Princess Ida who had some very advanced ideas about young women and their role in the world :

The garden fête at the opening of the Home for governesses, Kentish Town, North London, 12 June 1849. Inset: *The Home in Kentish Town, 1849.*

O lift your natures up:
Embrace our aims: work out your freedom. Girls,
Knowlege is now no more a fountain seal'd:
Drink deep, until the habits of the slave,
The sins of emptiness, gossip, and spite
And slander die. Better not be at all
Than not be noble.

Critics called it fantastic, but many believe that F. D. Maurice's ideas were only thinly disguised throughout the text and that Tennyson was probably preparing the way for the launch of Queen's College. In any event the speed at which plans were made and implemented was almost breathtaking: the first lectures were given in the summer of 1847; in July the nine professors involved formed a Committee of Education for the Institution; and in September a lease on the house next door to the Home in Harley Street was bought. The Committee of Education held its first formal meeting in October at the Marsden Library of King's College London, with F. D. Maurice as chairman; examinations took place in

35

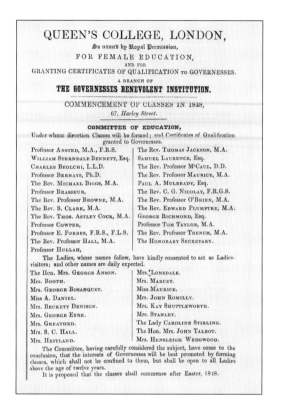

Notice announcing the Committee of Education of the GBI's proposal to commence classes at Queen's College London in 1848. 'The Committee [it announced] have come to the conclusion that the interests of Governesses will be best promoted by forming classes, which shall not be confined to them, but shall be open to all Ladies above the age of twelve years.'

December 1847, and the earliest certificates of academic competence that remain today in the archives were signed by David Laing on 23 December, naming Isabella Merritt and Matilda Mary Wallis Oxley.

At some time during this frenetic activity the Committee of Education decided to open up their experiment to all women instead of only governesses. F. D. Maurice was offered the job of Principal but declined, explaining that it 'could set me above my Colleagues at King's College'. He also felt that the job should go to someone who had a wife (his first wife, with whom he had lived so happily for seven years had died in 1845), with 'experience in education and be competent to exercise some control over pupils in the College'.

Maurice was adamant and remained Chairman of the Committee of Education. John Grigg, in his Queen's College Sesquicentenary lecture on F. D. Maurice, pointed out that Maurice must have relied heavily on Laing's practical experience and that there is evidence of the latter's irritation that all the credit for the founding of Queen's was going to Maurice.

At one point Frazer's *Magazine* carried this correction to an article on the College that it had published:

> Mr Laing desires us to state the Governesses' Benevolent Institution
> was in communication with the government and other parties respect-
> ing the establishment of the College as early as 1844, while there was
> no communication with the present professors until 1847; and that
> Her Majesty granted permission to use the royal name for the College
> before any connection was formed with the present Professors.

For his part Maurice is on record as having described Laing's conduct at
a meeting as fidgety and it is significant that in General Sir Frederick
Maurice's biography about his father, the name of Laing is not even
mentioned.

The matter of who would be called Principal was shelved in 1847. No
Principal was appointed at that time, but it was clearly a moment in the
history of the Institution when the leadership passed from the
redoubtable David Laing to Professor Maurice, who, in later years, would
become known as 'The Founder' of Queen's College.

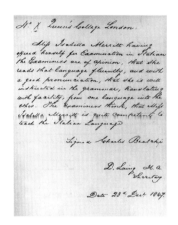

*The earliest certificate of
academic competence
awarded by Queen's
College to a Miss Isabella
Merritt in 1847, and
signed by David Laing.*

F. D. Maurice, 1805–72, Professor of Theology at King's College London from 1846 to 1853, and from 1866 Professor of Moral Philosophy at Cambridge. He was founder and first principal of the Working Men's College and founder of Queen's College, Harley Street.

CHAPTER FOUR

THE FOUNDER

The teachers of a school may aim merely to impart information; the leaders of a College must lead their pupils to the apprehension of principles . . . study is not worth much if it is not busy about the roots of things.

F. D. MAURICE SET THE TONE FOR QUEEN'S COLLEGE in his inaugural speech at the Hanover Rooms in London on 29 March 1848. He couched his remarks carefully to allay the fears of those who had profound doubts about this pioneering enterprise. Already detractors had published snide remarks in the press and Maurice must have known that his scheme could easily unravel in the face of concerted criticisms.

He took the audience through the curriculum: English Literature and Grammar; Drawing; German, French, Italian, and Latin; Geography; History; Mechanics; Method in Teaching; Geology and Arithmetic. He made a special case for Mathematics, a subject for girls which he knew would draw unfavourable comment:

We have set down mathematics in our course for studies, knowing that we might thereby encounter the charge of giving a little learning which is dangerous, but being ready to meet that charge in this case as in others. We are aware that our pupils are not likely to advance far in mathematics, but we believe that if they learn really what they do

IT is proposed immediately after Easter to open a College in London for the Education of Females. The word 'College,' in this connexion has to English ears a novel and an ambitious sound. I wish we could have found a simpler which would have described our object as well. Since we have chosen this, we should take pains to explain the sense in which we use it; to show, if we can show truly, that we are not devising a scheme to realize some favourite theory, but are seeking, by humble and practical methods, to supply an acknowledged deficiency. For this purpose, and not that I may prove the superiority of our plan to all others, I have been requested to address you now.

Some years ago a Society was established for the assistance of Governesses. Its first object was to afford temporary relief to cases of great suffering; and second to cultivate provident habits in those who could afford to save anything out of their salaries; the third to raise annuities for those who were past work, and whose friends or former employers were unable or unwilling to support them. The necessity for the first and last of these efforts has been made painfully evident; the

The first page of F. D. Maurice's speech proposing the opening of a College for Females, delivered in the Hanover Rooms, London, on 29 March 1848.

Charles Kingsley, author of The Water Babies *and* Westward Ho! *and one of the first professors to lecture at Queen's College.*

learn, they will not have got what is dangerous but what is safe . . . and I cannot conceive that a young lady can feel her mind in a more dangerous state than it was because she has gained one truer glimpse in the conditions under which the world in which it has pleased God to place her actually exists.

Maurice could never be accused of using three words instead of thirty, but with patience it is possible to discern his meaning. In the same style he spoke about the ethos of the School and how it would be different from existing competitive and highly disciplined boys' public schools:

> The teacher in every department, if he does his duty, will admonish his pupils that they are not to make fashion, or public opinion, their rule; that they are not to draw or play, or to study arithmetic, or language or literature or history, in order to shine or be admired; that if these are their ends, they will not be sincere in their work or do it well.

To this day Queen's is not a hothouse of competition, and there are few prizes awarded in class or at the end of the academic year.

It is hard to imagine how different Queen's was from other schools at that time. The quality of the staff for example; some of the best scholars in the country agreed to lecture – many of them personal friends of Maurice. Although they were paid after the official opening of the College they continued to teach governesses free of charge in the late afternoons and evenings. Among the first professors in 1848 were: William Sterndale Bennett, a music teacher and composer who later

TIME TABLE. MICHAELMAS TERM, 1850.

HOUR OF COM- MENC- ING.	MONDAY. JUNIOR. 1.	2.	SENIOR. 1.	2.	TUESDAY. JUNIOR. 1.	2.	SENIOR. 1.	2.	WEDNESDAY. JUNIOR. 1.	2.	SENIOR. 1.	2.	THURSDAY. JUNIOR. 1.	2.	SENIOR. 1.	2.	FRIDAY. JUNIOR. 1.	2.	SENIOR. 1.	2.	SATURDAY. JUNIOR. 1.	2.	SENIOR. 1.	2.
10		German.	Moral Philosophy	Drawing— Landscape	Reading.		Drawing— Landscape		History— Ancient.	Method.	Theology. N.T.		Theology. N.T.	German.	Italian.			Drawing— Landscape	Method.		History— Ancient.	Arithmetic		Italian.
11¼	German.		German	Church History.	Drawing— Landscape	History— Ancient.	English Literature & History.				Geography		Latin.	German.		German.	Italian.	Reading.	Drawing— Landscape	English Literature & History.	Method.	History— Ancient.	Italian.	Algebra.
12½		Drawing— Figure.	Harmony.	German.	Vocal Music.	English History.		Church History.	French.			Geography	Drawing— Figure.		French.	Drawing— Figure.	Vocal Music.	English Grammar.	Drawing— Landscape			French.	History— Modern.	Reading.
1¾	Theology. O.T.	Drawing— Figure.		Harmony.	English Grammar.	Vocal Music.	Geometry.		Arithmetic.	French.	Natural Philosoph.	History— Modern.	Drawing— Figure.		Drawing— Figure.	French.	English History.	Vocal Music. Geography	Drawing— Landscape		Arithmetic.	Latin.	French.	History— Modern.
3		Theology. O.T.	Natural Philosoph.	Latin.		Vocal Music.			Geography	Arithmetic	History— Modern.			Drawing— Figure.	Natural Philosoph.			Vocal Music.	English Literature & History.		Latin.	French.	Arithmetic	
For Govern esses only.		History.				Geography.				Theory and Practice of Drawing.				English Language and Theology.				Algebra.						

Prayers will be read in the Library every Morning at a Quarter to Ten o'clock.

An early example of the school timetable.

became Principal of the Royal Academy of Music, the Revd Edward Plumptre, translator of Dante and later Dean of Wells (and incidentally Maurice's brother-in-law), the Revd Richard Chenevix Trench, the Dean of Westminster who was to be promoted to Archbishop of Dublin, the writer Charles Kingsley who taught English Literature and Composition, and Isidore Brasseur, tutor to the Prince of Wales, who taught French.

They arrived at the appointed time, gave their lecture, the girls took notes and the professors went back to their students at King's. It was more like the teaching of undergraduates at a university than at a school. Maurice and the Committee of Education were striving for girls to have access to higher education, some as young as 12. Clearly the younger girls were often out of their depth. The young ladies could even choose what they wanted to learn and they could sign up for individual lectures or take the full course. It was soon recognized that the younger ones needed extra help and in the following year a preparatory class was started in the mews at the back of the College.

The Waiting Room was where every day started. It was not considered decent, even at Queen's, for the young ladies to be without a chaperone when being taught, even when most of the professors had Reverend in front of their name. The Governesses' Institution had therefore to organize a committee of 'Lady Visitors' who took it in turns to sit in on the lectures and keep an eye on things.

There were some formidable women among them: the daughters of duchesses, wives of earls, middle-class women who were eager to see the reform of education; and the wife of the Viceroy of India. The swish of silk through the doors of Queen's went a long way to calming down the

Some of the influential first professors of Queen's College. Left: *Professor Sir William Sterndale Bennett, Professor of Harmony and Musical Composition at Queen's, also Professor of Music at Cambridge and Principal of the Royal Academy of Music from 1866;* middle: *the Revd E. Plumptre, Professor of Theology and Church History at Queen's, also Dean of Wells;* right: *the Revd Richard Chenevix Trench, Professor of Theology and Church History at Queen's, also Professor of Theology in King's College London, Dean of Westminster from 1856 and Archbishop of Dublin 1864–84.*

stuffier residents of Harley Street who feared that an experimental school in their midst might have an impact on property prices.

In the early years F. D. Maurice taught theology and history. One of his first pupils, Mary Hullah, recalled her memories of him at the Jubilee celebration of the College in 1898:

> Let me try to recall the scene at a Maurice lecture . . . The class room is large and bare; it is full of girls ranging from twenty to twelve years of age . . . there is a stillness in the room except for the scratching of pens and the sound of that beautiful voice that many of us remember. The professor sits behind table, and one hand ever in motion before his eyes. He talks to us without a book or note of history past or present, of literature, of men and women, divine love; sometimes he soars away from the subject in hand, and we follow the best we can, recognizing in part the truth that, face to face with genius, we are hearing of matters dear to the man and dear to God.

Maurice, as Principal, all but in name, of the new Queen's College, was almost a household name. He was one of the country's leading theologians with a long list of books to his credit. He was Professor of both English Literature and History at King's College London, and Chaplain to the influential Lincoln's Inn. He had coined the name Christian Socialism, and by the mid-1850s had also founded the Working Men's College. His friends and admirers called him 'The Prophet'.

It was no accident that Maurice became interested in education, and women's education in particular. He was born in 1805 into one of those English dissenting families that believed passionately in education. Frederick Denison Maurice grew up in the Manor House, at

Class photographs at the turn of the century.
Left: *the preparatory class for younger children, including boys, c.1904.*
Right: *girls in the mews, c.1900.*

The Waiting Room, Queen's College, where every day started. It is still an important venue for meetings, classes and chamber music.

Normanstone, near Lowestoft, the only son among five sisters and two orphaned children of one of Mrs Maurice's brothers. The father, Michael Maurice, a Unitarian clergyman, also ran a school, first at Normanstone and then at Clifton, near Bristol, in which the whole family were involved in teaching and caring.

Michael Maurice used a method which might be described as 'trickle down' in educating his own family. He tutored the older daughters and they in turn gave classes to their siblings, while Mr Maurice took sole charge of his only son's education. There was also a governess in the house while the children were growing up. The result was a lively family of independent-minded daughters who often surprised visitors to the house with their outspoken opinions.

Religion played an important part in Frederick's life. The Maurices had generations of Nonconformity in the family stretching back to the seventeenth century. But as Frederick was growing up his mother and his older sisters turned away from their father's Church and began to take an interest in other denominations, including those whose theology was Calvinist, and the established Church. The young Frederick was caught in

The Working Men's College,
Crowndale Road, Camden,
founded by F. D. Maurice
in 1854.

the middle of this schism and agonized for many years before he too left his father's Church to become a minister of the Church of England.

The shyness and conciliatory nature that was apparent throughout his life may well have sprung from that family crisis during his formative years.

Frederick went to Cambridge in 1823 where he read law. He shared those years with a group of brilliant young men including Alfred Tennyson, the future Poet Laureate and John Sterling, a future editor of *The Times*, Richard Chenevix Trench, destined to become Archbishop of Dublin, John Stuart Mill, who became an economist and worked tirelessly for women's emancipation, and Arthur Hallam, all of whom were to have a lasting influence on his life. They were all members of a club they called 'The Apostles', twelve young men who debated the sins of the world and how they would reorder political and economic life. Even at that time Maurice was writing about the need for a new approach to women's education in a magazine he started as an undergraduate.

He left Trinity College, Cambridge, without a degree in 1826. As Elaine Kaye explains: 'He gained a first in the Civil Law examinations, but in order to take the degree, he was required also to declare himself a member of the Church of England. Though he was now moving nearer to membership of that Church, he had not yet made up his mind, and he refused to commit himself; in turning his back on a degree, he was, as his father wrote to a friend, preserving his principles at the expense of his interest, for he was reasonably certain to have been offered a fellowship.'

After a stint in London, writing articles for literary magazines and editing *The Athenaeum*, he returned to full-time study, only this time at Exeter College, Oxford, where he gained a degree in theology and formed a determination to be ordained. He was baptized into the Church of England in 1831, and later that year began to work as a curate at a parish in Somerset, and later in Warwickshire.

Returning to London in 1836, he took the job of Chaplain to Guy's Hospital. Two years later he had moved on to the plum job of Chaplain at Lincoln's Inn where he built up a large following of admirers who flocked to hear him preach. By the time he had become interested in the Governesses' Benevolent Institution – probably brought along by his sister Mary – he was holding down two professorships at King's College London, and had published one of his most important theological books, *The Kingdom of Christ*.

One of the young men who helped to fill the chapel at Lincoln's Inn was the author of *Tom Brown's Schooldays*, Tom Hughes. With the experience still fresh in his memory he wrote in 1853:

> Very soon after Mr Maurice was appointed, the daily attendance at Chapel was crowded . . . I believe the daily congregation increased because when a man once got up and went to Chapel in the morning and heard Mr Maurice read the prayers, he felt there was somehow a reality about the service which was new to him, and he went again to satisfy his want; and if he overslept himself he found that he had lost something – that his day had not started right. At least that was my own case. If I missed morning chapel I had an uncomfortable feeling till eleven or twelve o'clock as if I had not had my breakfast or had put on a dirty shirt.

Tom Hughes went on to say that the hundreds who went to hear him on Sunday afternoons heard, 'a man speaking to them as men, sympathizing with them and not silencing them'. Maurice's close friend since Cambridge days, Alfred Tennyson, once remarked 'It is worth any sermon you could

Among the members of the 'Apostles' in F. D. Maurice's time were (top to bottom) *Alfred Lord Tennyson, the future Poet Laureate, Arthur Henry Hallam* (sketch for a bust by Sir Francis Chantrey, 1781–1841) *and John Stuart Mill* (painting by George Frederic Watts, 1873).

preach to hear Maurice read the Lord's Prayer. His belief in God's presence was so intense that familiar prayers took on new fire and meaning.'

But there were some who found Maurice difficult to comprehend. Even the well-disposed future Prime Minister William Gladstone (one of Maurice's sisters was companion to Gladstone's sister) found the 'Prophet's' theology, 'a good deal of an enigma'. And according to Alec R. Vidler's book *Maurice and Company*, contemporaries commented, 'Maurice has been petted and told that he is a philosopher, till he naturally thinks he is one, and he has not a clear idea in his head.' There were other equally mystified people who could not get a grip on Maurice's line of thought and according to Dr Vidler:

> He cannot be satisfactorily classified, and this is one reason why his teaching has been regarded as mystifying . . . None of the labels that have been proposed really sticks to him. The label that has come closest to sticking in popular reputation is Christian Socialist, but it is necessary only to read his biography, or scan the list of his published works, in order to perceive that albeit significant in its way, it covers only a small segment of his interests and does not serve to identify him.

Maurice must have had a frantic life in the 1840s, churning out sermons for Guy's and Lincoln's Inn, writing his theological books, lecturing at King's College and attending committee meetings of the Governesses. But despite this workload, he had begun to get involved with the working-class Chartist movement that took its name from a charter of 1838 in which the organizers called for annual parliaments; universal male suffrage; the ballot; no property qualifications for Members of Parliament; payment of Members; and equal electoral districts. The landowning and middle classes were alarmed, and the movement was suppressed. But in the 1840s, when revolution toppled governments in many other parts of Europe, and Karl Marx and Engels founded the Communist League in London, the Chartists tried again to push the government towards reform. In April, during the run-up to the official opening of Queen's, Maurice, the social campaigner John Ludlow, and Charles Kingsley, were preparing to launch a newspaper to reflect the political and social issues behind the tumultuous call for change. Men from all over England were marching on London. People were very edgy and the military was mobilized. But in the event the march was halted south of the Thames and the petition for reform was driven to Parliament in three hansom cabs.

Less than a year after launching Queen's Maurice set up another school in a yard near his house in Queen's Square. Little Ormond Yard, he was told, was 'so disorderly that no policeman liked to venture there at night', but Maurice was determined to open a night school for men that was clearly the genesis of the Working Men's College which he later founded. The school in Little Ormond Yard, however, became so popular among young boys that the men drifted away, mothers brought more and more boys, and Maurice had to pay for a teacher to help him. Characteristically he added a girls' class and hired a second teacher. Friends helped out and to ensure everyone's safety there was a rule that no teacher or organizer should work there alone! One night Maurice ignored his own advice and in trying to keep order had to throw out one of the trouble-makers.

Another very practical scheme took shape in 1850, as L. M. Dean explained in her unpublished biography of Maurice: 'The scheme was to form associations of different trades, the members to work together, manage their own affairs, sell direct, avoiding middlemen and competition . . . the (Council's) constitution was provided for any body of workmen who wished to form an association, and as much as could be was done to protect the men until a modification was obtained of the existing law on partnership.' There were associations of tailors, builders, printers, bakers, smiths, pianoforte makers, and also a needlewomen's guild. But as the movement grew Maurice had to face the suspicion that he was turning into a rabble-rouser under a cloak of so-called Christian Socialism. He was obliged to explain his views to the Principal of King's College:

> We certainly believe that socialism . . . if it were based upon Christianity, might be the most powerful protection of the land against anarchical notions and practices . . . We know that by so doing we have led some workmen to see the folly and danger of strikes, that we have provoked the hostility of many incendiaries, that we have especially offended those who were using the distresses of the lower orders as arguments of infidelity. I believe that the fact that a clergyman holding office in your college is connected with them has helped to diminish some prejudices which a portion of the working class entertained against this order, and to make their minds more ready for the reception of Christian teaching.

Octavia Hill, one of the founders of the National Trust. She was a devoted disciple of F. D. Maurice. Her sister took two Latin certificates at Queen's in 1863 and 1864, and married F. D. Maurice's son.

In 1851 Maurice toured Lancashire to spread the message of the associations and some were started among the cotton workers. In London he organized meetings and Bible readings at his house – early morning meetings were called 'prophetic breakfasts' – for all those interested in Christian Socialism. One major obstacle that Maurice and his colleagues were able to clear was the legal block to working men owning property. After several years of framing new legislation and lobbying ministers, a bill was put through Parliament that cleared the way for the founding of the Co-operative Movement.

However, Maurice's credentials as a 'socialist' need careful scrutinizing in the context of middle-class mid-nineteenth century ideas about socialism. Historian John Grigg, in his Queen's sesquicentenary lecture on Maurice in November 1997, entitled his lecture, 'F. D. Maurice – Reluctant Radical':

> In Maurice's view the purpose of the state was to preserve individual rights and property. He was opposed to democracy, except in the most limited and qualified sense. He could approve of state intervention to protect factory children, but even in such instances felt that the state was 'going out of its own sphere'. In principle, the only sort of collective action that he approved was voluntary. Moreover, the Utilitarian creed was anathema to him. Society could flourish only under God, and through a recognition of God's law as revealed in Christ. If people would behave to each other in a Christian way, accepting class distinctions, harmony would prevail. He was against trade unions for the same reason that he was against political parties – that they were divisive. He was also against economic and every other sort of competition. Christian co-operation was his ideal.

One of the associations that Maurice set up, the Needlewomen's Guild, failed, but he was determined to salvage what he could. He got them to start on other work, painting on glass. As L. M. Dean explained, Octavia Hill, one of the future founders of the National Trust, became involved:

> A house was taken in Little Charlotte Street and Mrs Hill lived there and supervised the work while her daughter Octavia did the teaching ... Octavia Hill was his devoted disciple, and the wonderful work she did in property management derives directly from him. Perhaps the easiest way to fathom Maurice's ideas is to study them as they were worked out practically in the slum property managed by Octavia.

Certainly neither would have approved of the Welfare State as we know it, for people were always people, not cases or numbers, and they were trained to help themselves. Octavia Hill knew how terrible were the living conditions of the poor, and her great desire to improve them led to the celebrated Victorian artist John Ruskin buying a block of tenements in Paradise Place, Marylebone, and letting her manage them. Gradually her property was a shining example of what could be done when there are friendly relations between landlord and tenant.

Meanwhile the management committees of both King's and Queen's Colleges had become increasingly uneasy about the bad press that Maurice and Charles Kingsley were receiving for their espousal of Christian Socialism. Personal attacks on their integrity were printed in the *Quarterly Review*, an influential literary journal, saying that they were clever, but wayward-minded men, and that Christian Socialism was certainly suspect. Worse than that, Maurice wrote some theological essays in which he set out his views on the concept of eternal damnation. He challenged the Church's traditional teaching, and the charge of heresy was whispered. At this distance it is hard to know what all the fuss was about and Maurice hardly made it clear in his writings what he meant. This is how he tried to explain himself in a letter to another clergyman:

> I never dreamed of merging time in eternity. The phrases which suggest such a thought belong to the popular theology and seem to be most unsatisfactory. I maintain that time and eternity coexist. Here the difficulty is to recognize the eternal state under our temporal conditions; not to lose identity in time. We must someday know that we are living and moving and having our being in God; we cannot always act upon the strange lie that the things which we see are those that determine what we are but although I may speak of death as bringing us acquainted with eternity, face to face, I have no business, as far as I see at present, to speak of death as ending time.

The governing Council of King's College, embarrassed by Maurice's 'left-wing' politics and his theology, voted to dismiss him. They did so with immediate effect in November 1853. Maurice's friends and many fellow academics objected but the governing board stood firm.

Alfred Tennyson, by this time Poet Laureate, had asked Maurice to be godfather to his son, wrote a rousing poem to show his support:

Come, when no graver cares employ,
Godfather, come and see your boy:
Your presence will be sun in Winter,
Making the little one leap for joy.

For, being of that honest few
Who give the Fiend himself his due,
Should eighty thousand College councils
Thunder, 'Anathema', friend, at you;

Should all our churchmen foam in spite
At you, so careful of the right,
Yet one lay-hearth would give you welcome
(Take it and come) to the Isle of Wight.

At Queen's Maurice insisted on resigning his chairmanship of the Committee of Education, but agreed to stay on as a lecturer, given the unanimous support of the governing Council. Some members, fearful for the survival of the College, voted against Maurice staying on and that was that. King's College Council had thundered 'Anathema' at him and had dismissed 'the Prophet'. He had made it too easy for the doubters and detractors at Queen's, and had virtually allowed himself to be dismissed.

Today it seems extraordinary that he chose not to ride out the storm of fear and petty-mindedness; perhaps it was an echo of his childhood dread of dissension and conflict about religion. Maurice's letter of resignation is choked with sadness:

I am thankful that the sharp pain which it costs me to sever a connection so affectionate and cordial as ours has been, will not be increased by the reflection that the College will be the sufferer. Previously to the appointment of a Council even a single withdrawal might have shaken you; now I trust you will become stronger every day. My Moral Philosophy class though it has increased this term is still the smallest in the College; in Literature I was merely acting as Strettel's substitute. The office of Chairman you will be able to supply admirably, even if the zeal and efficiency of the excellent deputy did not make it now, as it has always been a very easy office. What a pleasant one your confidence has made it, I do not trust myself to say even in a letter; I had not the courage to tell you in person this evening.

It was three years before Maurice was invited back to lecture. He was not, however, destined to take up the reigns of leadership again, and although he gave lectures at Queen's for another ten years his name crops up only infrequently during a time of change and turmoil in the world of women's education. It might be true to say that Maurice was the best Principal Queen's never had.

Maurice did not retreat into educational history as an embittered tragic figure. He was just as busy with his writing and preaching and was able to give more time to the cause of working-class education. The Working Men's College was founded by him in 1854. He threw himself into the administration and the teaching, and agreed to be installed as Principal after a delegation of tradesmen and craftsmen arrived with a petition imploring him to take the job. In 1856 he turned his attention to setting up the Working Women's College. Octavia Hill gave lectures on arithmetic and old friends from the staff at Queen's College, such as the celebrated singing teacher and composer John Hullah, also took classes at the new College. In 1866 Maurice was reinstated as a leading academic when he accepted the chair of Professor of Theology and Philosophy at Cambridge, where he continued writing and preaching until his death in 1872. He was buried in the family vault at Highgate Cemetery in London where his name can still be seen carved in the base of the white cross that marks the vault.

F. D. Maurice, c. 1865.

Girls dressed for a Greek play at Queen's, 1886. Clockwise from top left: *Ethel Pilcher, Grace David, Margaret Dodson, Nelly Birrell, Violet Dewey.*

CHAPTER FIVE

'CRINOLINES AND CHAPERONES'

I was the very first pupil at Queen's College School. I was just about nine, low frock and short sleeves and curls. I had heard about Queen's College at home and I rather liked the idea of going, only I fancied one hour for one subject would be very long.

MARY HULLAH, PROBABLY THE DAUGHTER of the Music Professor, recalled the day she turned up at the preparatory class which opened one year after the College in 1849. It was one of many developments that the Committee of Education, under Maurice's chairmanship, put in hand. Right at the start it became apparent that some sort of preparation would be needed for the very young ladies who were supposed to be able to take in lectures aimed at a much older age group. 'On the first day that the School opened I went and waited all day and nobody else came, so as there was no teaching, I think I amused myself with books in the library.' Mary and her sister Caroline were joined by four other pioneering pupils who were given lessons, firstly by 'Professor Cock in the bay window of the waiting room, Miss Parry presiding'. Later classes moved upstairs to the second-floor rooms.

By the following year the preparatory class had attracted forty-two girls and by 1852 it was offering a three-year course for pupils from the age of 9 to 14, including a limited number of boys. By the time the class became known officially as Queen's College School, new accommodation

Queen's College School, 1907. First called the preparatory class, the School was founded in 1849. Boys as well as girls attended the School.

had been found in the stables at the back of Harley Street. There is no sign of the first schoolrooms today. They were swept away, along with some workshops and little houses when the present 'yellow' block, with its gymnasium, was built. In the nineteenth century most of the children were in one large room with the classes divided by curtains. 'The Headmistress of the School (Miss Parry) had a sanctum behind a red and black brocade curtain, in the same room as the top class.'

The preparatory-class children were taught arithmetic, drawing, grammar, French, German, geography, history, Latin, music, natural history, reading, and writing, between the hours of 9.30 and 12.30. The fees were 6 guineas a term or 15 guineas a year.

Some of the classes in the converted stables were taken by professors but unlike the College, the tutors and assistants were all women. The second Headmistress, Miss Hay, was appointed in 1857 and stayed until 1893, and, if her former students are to be believed, was a wonderful character who had a great influence on all the children. One of her pupils, Olivia Garnett, recalled 'a stout figure puffing and blowing along the corridor to take her class. She must have been a nature lover, for of her I chiefly remember the vistas she occasionally opened during lessons into foreign climes as, casting up her eyes, while bugles in her cap shook and gleamed, she quoted with a thrill in her voice: "With thy cornfields green and sunny vines, Oh pleasant land of France." '

It must have been Miss Hay who seized the opportunity to start a kindergarten class in 1860 when a teacher called Rosa Hosking returned from abroad having studied the Pestalozzi teaching method. By 1878 the School was teaching over 170 pupils and when it was examined by the Cambridge Syndicate in the 1870s and 1880s it was consistently praised for the good job it was doing.

The introduction of a preparatory class at Queen's in 1849 was only one of many projects in which the Committee of Education was involved. Despite the pioneering challenge they faced in getting Queen's launched, the professors and the GBI Council approved the idea of setting up a 'City' branch of Queen's College. Two more committees were formed – one in Harley Street and a 'local' committee in the City of which Miles Beale, the father of Dorothea Beale, was a member. A house was rented at 4 Artillery Place and the City branch of Queen's opened on 30 January 1850.

But Harley Street and the local committee fell out over the appointment of professors. The City committee unilaterally elected men of their choice and asked for self-government. In December 1850 the 'City' asked for permission to be known as Queen's College in the City and were refused. The 'City' then went its own way calling itself 'City of London College for Ladies'. As far as we know Harley Street did not encourage any further connection as the minutes of the GBI are silent after 1851, and the last mention of this school in the 'City Directory' at Guildhall Library is 1886.

Soon after its inception Queen's College itself had been considering separation from the parent Governesses' Benevolent Institution, and in 1853, just after F. D. Maurice's untimely resignation, the College received its own charter and total independence from the Institution that founded it. Physically, very little changed. The GBI Home for governesses, set up in 1847, remained where it was, in what is now

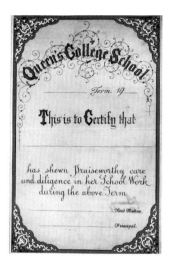

Certificates were given to show that pupils had completed their classes.

The Revd Charles Grenfell Nicolay, one of the first professors at Queen's. He took over the responsibility of day-to-day administration after F. D. Maurice resigned in 1853.

47 Harley Street, and the College continued to teach free of charge those governesses staying in the Home. The GBI continued to provide the Home for unemployed governesses alongside the houses occupied by Queen's College until 1923 when the GBI moved the Home to 8 Cavendish Street.

A new governing Council for Queen's, made up of the great, the good, and the aristocratic, was set up with the Bishop of London as the 'Visitor', the figurehead to whom, if all else failed, a grievance could be taken. Bishops of London have retained this relationship with the College for a century and a half. The governing Council today consists of seventeen men and eleven women with a wide range of interests: education, trade unionism, accountancy, banking, medicine, and in some cases, just a general interest in education and the well-being of the College. In May 1991 the Council decided to encourage parents of girls at Queen's to take part in its deliberations, and to invite two parents to become members of the Council.

In 1853, when the College, with its own charter, became independent of the Governesses' Benevolent Institution, the biggest upset was the departure of Maurice. For the rest it was business as usual. Maurice's successor as Chairman and Principal was Richard Chenevix Trench, a professor at King's and, after 1856, the Dean of Westminster. A year later Chenevix Trench was appointed Archbishop of Dublin and on taking up his post he established Alexandra College, Dublin, in the image of Queen's College. In Harley Street, most of the original members of the GBI Committee of Education transferred their allegiance to Queen's, and one of them, Charles Grenfell Nicolay, who was also the Chaplain and Librarian at King's College, took over the day-to-day running of Queen's. One of the founder members of the Committee of Education, he lectured in geography at both King's and Queen's, and, according to Camilla Croudace, a former student and later Lady Resident, Nicolay's organization of the teaching and the classes was impeccable: 'So well had he thought out the curriculum, that any departure from his rules had been found, after trial, to have been a mistake.' He was, however, far from popular with the Lady Visitors. They objected to his habit of interviewing pupils in the absence of either a chaperone or their mother. Moreover he lived upstairs with his family of eight children including his eldest son aged 14. The Lady Visitors felt that the boy could become a moral threat to the young ladies. The Council declared their trust in Nicolay and twenty-one Lady Visitors

The arrival of Queen Victoria at Queen's College on its Golden Jubilee, May 1898. The painting by the drawing teacher Ella Bedford hangs today in the stairwell of 45 Harley Street.

resigned. A year later in 1856 Nicolay left Queen's to take up a post of Chaplain in Bahia, South America.

Obtaining the new charter was so expensive that the professors of the new Committee all generously agreed to underwrite the cost of acquiring their new independent status, and Maurice, even though he had by this time resigned, contributed his share of £200.

In 1854 the festival of 'Annual Gathering' was held for the first time, one of several traditions which is still maintained. The Bishop of London comes to the College to listen to the Principal's report, and to meet the girls in the College who are all dressed in white. Occasionally some try to kick over the traces by turning up in dresses that are distinctly off-white, or slightly diaphanous, while many of the younger ones insist that their laced-up 'Doc Martens' boots are right for any occasion. The girls and the staff line up to meet the Visitor in the floral splendour of the main corridor that leads to the Pfeiffer Hall. The Bishop greets each girl as he progresses through the School, up the staircase and past the painting of Maurice on the landing, and into the Hall, where the Principal delivers a rousing report on the College's activity throughout the year, followed by the Bishop's thoughts on the meaning of life.

The Bishop's visit was an annual event, as it is today, but the professors from King's College were in weekly, if not daily, contact with the girls who crammed through the doors of number 45 Harley Street in their crinolines and bonnets.

> We may imagine our young ladies accompanied by a mother or domestic attendant [wrote Rosalie Grylls in *Queen's College 1848–1948*] moving along the street towards the College doors with the soberness necessarily imposed by the weight of their long, full skirts held out by at least seven petticoats (one of which would have been flame red) and mounting the steps a little tremulous as to what awaited them. They would have been met by the Lady Resident whose job it was to deal with the domestic side of the College.

The first pupil on the first day, Sarah Woodman, who went on to become a governess to the 'upper classes', recalled her encounter with Mrs Mattam:

> How useful in her generation was that esteemed first Lady Resident. Mrs Mattam possessed of no intellectual power nor of much organizing

Facing page: Queen's College as it looks today.

Lucy Baldwin-Ridsdale, a distinguished Lady Visitor who chaperoned the girls at Queen's.

Arthur Penrhyn Stanley, Dean of Westminster, who was Principal of Queen's College from 1863 to 1872.

The Revd J. Llewelyn Davies, Principal of Queen's 1873–4 and 1879–86. He was the brother of Emily Davies, a former student of Queen's who went on to found Girton College, Cambridge.

capability, yet she proved herself to be the right person in the right place, for she seemed by her almost maternal line of action, at least to understand the necessity of the moment, namely to become the connecting link between the professors and the girls, for, though I say it with bated breath, I humbly believe that the professors were quite as much afraid of the girl pupils as the girl pupils were of them.

The Lady Resident, of whom there were many talented and formidable ones in later years, introduced the young ladies to the Lady Visitors who then sat in on the lectures as chaperones.

Many of the pupils in the early years were local to the College, according to the lists of students that have survived in the archives, with addresses like Wimpole and Harley Streets, St John's Wood, and Hampstead. Their fathers were usually well-off, well-established men whose occupations ranged from medicine and landowning to serving Her Majesty as officers in the army. Queen's was definitely middle and upper-middle class, but with a sprinkling of the daughters of better-off merchants and tradesmen.

The Lady Visitors wrote everything down in a leather-bound book with a brass lock. It survives today in the archives with its lock long broken and secrets revealed. Lessons, which started at 10.00 a.m. and ended at 3.00 p.m., overlapped with no break for tea or lunch, Monday to Saturday, so there was little opportunity for girls of different social backgrounds to mix. By the end of the first year the professors were giving lectures to 250 pupils.

Maurice was not the only professor to leave a marked impression on the minds of the young ladies. Sarah Woodman recalled her lessons in the College Jubilee Book of 1898:

How vividly I recall the scholarly Latin teaching of Professor Clark, the philosophical language lectures of Professor Bernays and A. B. Strettle, the marvellous patience of Professor Brasseur in correcting faults of accent acquired in previous years, the racy spirit-inspiring lectures of the Revd J. S. Brewer on Modern History, the ample illustrations of Professor O'Bryan's scientific lectures, and, though last but by no means least, the enthusiastic heart-stirring appeals of the Principal of Battersea Training College, Dr Thomas Jackson, on the art of teaching.

Another favourite professor who opened up the mysteries of science to girls was the Revd Professor Thomas Astley Cock, who, with his own money, bought much of the scientific equipment he needed for the lectures. 'Mr Astley Cock was one of the most humorous and amusing people one could find,' Alice Heale (1876–80) warmly recalled:

> He had the most eccentric habits and was very witty and most sarcastic. He did not mind how he looked – he would enter the room and place an exceedingly shabby little bag on a kind of a counter and from it during class would draw out grubby little screws of paper, containing tea, a few lumps of sugar and a slice or two of uninviting bread and butter, and while the girls were working out a problem he would slowly munch his repast eyeing the class with a humorous twinkle.

Revd E. H. Plumptre started teaching at Queen's in 1848, became Principal in 1875 and retired in 1879.

He taught mathematics at Queen's for thirty-five years and resigned in 1883 only because the Lady Visitors and the Cambridge examiners of the day began to complain about his teaching. The centre table in the Senior Library is carved in his memory: 'To the honoured memory of Rev. Thomas Astley Cock Professor at Queen's College from its foundation in 1848 to his death July 3rd 1885 and gladly wolde he lerne, and gladly teche' – a quotation from Chaucer's *Canterbury Tales*. Alice Heale also mentions some members of the domestic staff such as Alphonse, the French pantry boy and a general handyman called Catchpole:

Revd Thomas Astley Cock taught mathematics at Queen's for thirty-five years and was much loved by the students. He is remembered today by a memorial table in the Senior Library.

> He wore a very poor livery, plumb buttons in the afternoon; he was about 35 or 40 I should think, very polite and obliging, but I never saw him smile. He was very dignified. Mr Astley Cock poked fun at him in the Natural Philosophy class where he was sometimes required to hold some vessel or other necessary to the experiment in hand . . . I see him now with a large vase-shaped copper container full of coal on his arm making splendid fires which burnt the faces of those in the front desks and left shivering the poor things in the back rows.

The Revd E. H. Plumptre was another favourite in the College. Like his colleagues at King's he managed to combine his job as Professor of Theology with the new challenge presented by the founding of Queen's College. He was married to Harriet, one of F. D. Maurice's sisters, and joined his brother-in-law on the Committee of Education at Queen's in 1848. As well as teaching he took on the job of Dean of Queen's College.

Certificate of Associateship, 1877, awarded to a Miss Annette Dalton and signed by H. Craik, Dean, and G. H. Plumptre, Principal.

Caricature of Charles Kingsley by Adriano Cecioni (1838–86).

Camilla Croudace, a former student who later became a Lady Resident of great distinction, was struck by Plumptre's appearance. 'He had a very Roman face. His manner was shy but at the same time genial and kind. He inspired a wholesome awe as it was a very serious thing to be reported to the Dean.' There is a reference in the archives to him walking from Gloucester Road to Harley Street every day 'mentally translating Dante'.

Another student whose reminiscences are also in the archives has left us a clear image of him at work:

> He was very quick and active, used to run upstairs and always taught standing, his tall slight figure swaying from side to side he leaned first on one foot and then on the other . . . his lectures were delivered in a high-pitched vibrating rather monotonous voice. He spoke quietly, continuously, he asked no questions . . . though he called in our notebooks and gave examinations every term.

Towards the end of his career in 1875 he was appointed Principal – a post he held until 1879. Soon after retiring from Queen's, the Prime Minister William Gladstone invited him to become Dean of Wells in 1882.

Charles Kingsley, the author of *The Water Babies* and *Westward Ho!*, was a more controversial professor at Queen's. As Rector of Eversley he admired Maurice's writings and became acquainted with him in 1844 – he referred to him as his 'master' – and, when Queen's was launched in 1848, Maurice appointed him Professor of English Literature. Together, throughout that turbulent year, they had worked to improve employment and living conditions for the working classes in the movement that became known as Christian Socialism. Kingsley helped Maurice start the short-lived magazine *Politics for the People* and among many other topics contributed articles about the National Gallery: 'Picture galleries should be the work, man's paradise, and garden of pleasure, to which he goes to refresh his eyes and heart with beautiful shapes and sweet colouring, when they are weary with bricks and mortar and other colourless things which fill the workshop and factory.'

He cared deeply about the poor and the conditions in which they lived and worked. Housing for labourers in parts of London were known as 'rookeries', so overcrowded and insanitary were the conditions. It was only in June 1847, the year before Queen's opened its doors, that Parliament passed an Act limiting the working day of women and teenage children to 10 hours. Kingsley believed in women having access to higher education

and was especially interested in giving women the opportunity to study medicine. As we discovered in Chapter 4 his opinions were considered dangerous – even the teaching of young women at Queen's to write poetry. But what lively events his lectures must have been if this letter to a fellow professor at Queen's is anything to go by:

> We want to train – not cupboards full of 'information' (vile misnomer) – but real informed women.
>
> Don't be afraid of talking about marriage. We must be real and daring at Queen's College, or nowhere. The clear stage and no favour

Queen's College boarders, c. 1880. They lived on the top floors of the College buildings under the supervision of Clara Wood.

61

which we have got there is so blessed and wonderful an opening, that we must make the most of it to utter things there which prudery and fanaticism have banished form pulpits and colleges.

Sadly Kingsley taught for only one year at Queen's.

The professors at Queen's were happy to promote other educational enterprises as well, the new school called the Ladies' College, Bedford Square, for example, which opened one year after Queen's. It was started in that almost perfect Georgian square on the Bedford estate by Mrs Elizabeth Jesser Reid who was also a keen supporter of Queen's. She wanted, however, a college for women which was not only independent of the established Church, but also an institution that was governed by women for women. Maurice would have nothing to do with it because one of the prime movers – Francis Newman, Professor of Latin at University College – was considered to be a 'freethinker' who had rejected much of conventional Christian teaching.

Other professors from Queen's, including John Hullah and Sterndale Bennett, did give lectures. Some of Queen's Lady Visitors included Bedford College in their weekly round of duties and a former pupil of Queen's, Frances Martin, was recruited to be the governess of the preparatory classes which started in 1853.

Dorothea Beale was another educational pioneer, whose school, the Cheltenham Ladies' College, had a profound effect on sound academic education for girls. Dorothea attended Queen's in 1849, and, as she described in the Queen's College Jubilee Book, stayed for seven years:

> I can perhaps scarcely claim to have been a pupil of Queen's, seeing that I attended only one class for a short time, until after I had become a teacher. In 1849 I had joined Mr Cock's class for mathematics, but as this was elementary, and I had read a good deal alone, I found private lessons necessary; he soon after asked me to help in teaching and I was appointed the first lady mathematical tutor . . . In 1853 I was appointed Latin tutor, and a little later was offered the post of head teacher in the School under Miss Parry.

She left in 1856 to become head teacher at the Clergy School in Casterton and a year later moved to the recently founded Cheltenham Ladies' College where, as Principal, her writ was law for a remarkable forty years.

Dorothea Beale, who attended Queen's in 1849 principal of Cheltenham Ladies' College and founder of St Hilda's College, Oxford.

Frances Mary Buss was another teacher whose contribution to improving the education of women was immense. She was a young teacher who attended lectures at Queen's and went on to head the school that she and her mother founded in 1850, the North London Collegiate School for Girls. In one of her letters to Dorothea Beale she explains how she was a beneficiary of David Laing's policy of giving evening courses for working governesses and teachers:

Frances Mary Buss in 1890. A student at Queen's College, she later founded the North London Collegiate School for Girls.

> Mr Laing kept to his original idea and soon induced some of the professors to give, free of charge, courses of evening lectures to women actually engaged in teaching. Mr Cock took arithmetic, Mr Brewer Latin translation – he was a first-rate teacher . . . Mr Laing gave scripture. The first term I attended six nights a week, the second four . . . Queen's College opened a new life to me, I mean intellectually. To come in contact with the minds of such men was indeed delightful, and it was a new experience to me.

Both Buss and Beale became legends in their own lifetime and were famous enough for this anonymous ditty to have been universally chanted:

> Miss Buss and Miss Beale
> Cupid's darts do not feel;
> How different from us,
> Miss Beale and Miss Buss!

It is hard to quantify the influence that spread out across the British Isles from the educational experiment that started at Queen's. The professors had caught the beginning of a wave of public interest in the subject and in the following decades England was dotted with girls' schools where former Queen's students were either teaching or controlling. Many took jobs with the Girls' Public Day School Company, which became a Trust in 1906 and survives today as the Girls' Day School Trust with dozens of schools under its aegis. By the end of the nineteenth century the Company had opened over thirty non-denominational high schools. The Church of England had launched almost as many, and over ninety girls' grammar schools were also offering an academic education. Queen's had touched them all in some measure.

Sophia Jex-Blake, one of the pioneers in women's medicine. She studied at Queen's in 1858 and later taught mathematics there from 1859 to 1861.

Alice Bishop, at Harley Street from 1858 to 1863, had a career as Headmistress for new schools set up by the Girls' Public Day School Company. Alice's sister Matilda (1858–60) became Headmistress of Kensington High School and later the first Principal of Royal Holloway College; Dame Frances Dove (1860–2) was Headmistress of St Leonard's School, St Andrews, before founding Wycombe Abbey School in Buckinghamshire, 1896. Dame Frances returned to Queen's towards the end of her career in 1909 to take her turn at being a Lady Visitor; Frances Martin, after helping with the foundation of Bedford College, went on to work with F. D. Maurice in the founding of the College for Working Women in 1864 in Queen's Square, Bloomsbury.

The science at Queen's in the early days was an important feature. It was rare for girls to be taught science well anywhere else, and the study of medicine, almost a taboo subject for women at the time when Queen's was founded, caught the imagination of many young women. Sophia Jex-Blake was among them. She became a celebrity during her pioneering battles with the medical establishment. She was at Queen's in 1858 as a student and stayed to become an assistant to the mathematics professor from 1859 to 1861.

After a visit to America, where she met several women doctors, she returned home eager to scale the bastions of male prejudice that kept the 'bluestockings' on the outside of the world of medicine. In her contribution to the Queen's Jubilee Book of 1898 she explained that while the Medical Act of 1858 had apparently opened the way for women to become doctors in Britain, the nineteen different licensing bodies involved were under no obligation to examine women. It meant that in the late 1850s only one woman doctor was on the medical register, the English-born Elizabeth Blackwell, who graduated from a New York State college in 1849. Elizabeth Garrett Anderson, another pioneer doctor, who under the name Elizabeth Garrett attended lectures at Queen's as a young woman and, later, in the 1880s, was a member of the Council of Queen's; she was the first woman to qualify as a doctor of medicine in Britain.

Elizabeth Garrett Anderson was examined by the Society of Apothecaries in London, received her qualification in 1866, and opened a small dispensary for women and children in Marylebone. A major influence in opening up the medical profession to women, she built the New Hospital for Women in London which after her death was renamed the Elizabeth Garrett Anderson Hospital. At the time she was recognized by the General Medical Council there were then only two women doctors in the whole of the British Isles, but, as Sophia Jex-Blake explained, the medical establishment then pulled down the shutters on future applicants:

> The door, however, thus opened was speedily closed, for the medical world was indignant at Miss Garrett's success, and when two more women passed the preliminary examination in Arts, with a view to following in her steps, the authorities of the Apothecaries Hall 'bethought them to invent a rule forbidding students to receive any part of their medical education privately', this course being publicly advised by one of the medical journals as a safe way of avoiding their legal obligations, and shutting out the one chance left to women.

Sophia Jex-Blake recruited three other women who wanted to study medicine and applied to the University of Edinburgh in 1869. After some consideration the University agreed that although the women could be given instruction, it had to be in a special women's class which cost considerably more. The women all excelled in their exams, one even qualifying for a scholarship which was denied because she had not been part of the main class – which, of course, was an all-male affair. Already Sophia and her small group had made history by becoming the first women undergraduates to study full time in a British university. Alarmed by the women's success, and the disturbing proof that their brains were not hampered by size, the male students began a campaign to banish them from the University. Fearing that the granting of degrees to women would in some way discount the value of their own qualification, they ganged up on the women when they arrived for the beginning of the next university term. A crowd of young men stood in their way and shouted obscenities while pelting them with fruit and vegetables, in an attempt to stop them getting to the lectures. The University authorities backed down and despite years of appeal the women were forced to concede defeat. The would-be doctors retreated south and with sympathetic members of the medical profession in London, founded the London School of Medicine for Women in 1874. Sophia, who ran the administration, had still to qualify as a physician. The breakthrough came in Dublin when the Irish College of Physicians and Queen's University of Ireland agreed to admit women for examination and diplomas. Sophia and three others took the Dublin examination, and, in 1877, their names were added to the register of the General Medical Council.

Elizabeth Garrett Anderson, who attended lectures at Queen's, was the first woman to qualify as a doctor of medicine in Britain. She is seen here taking her doctoral exam.

Gertrude Bell (student at Queen's, 1882–6) is commemorated with a bust in the main corridor of the College. The bust is a replica of one placed in the Baghdad Museum in a wing dedicated by King Feisal to her memory and was presented to Queen's College by her cousin Horace Marshall.

Emily Davies, founder of Girton College.

At the celebrations of the fiftieth anniversary of the founding of Queen's College Sophia Jex-Blake was able to report, 'At the end of 1877 there were seven women registered as medical practitioners, at the end of 1897 the number was three hundred and forty-five; a large number of those hold appointments in hospitals, asylums and workhouse infirmaries in this country and about a hundred are working (as medical missionaries or otherwise) in India, China, and other foreign lands.'

Among those successful medicos was Louisa Bovell Sturge (1855–60), who completed her studies in Paris, and returned to London to be a physician at the new hospital for women in Marylebone Road. She also gave lectures at Queen's in physiology and hygiene. One of the laboratories at Queen's today is named after her and in the Senior Library there is a bookcase with her portrait, and that of her sister Emily, carved into the wooden doors. Later in the nineteenth century another former Queen's student, Eleanor Davies-Colley, became the first woman to be elected a fellow of the Royal College of Surgeons.

Gertrude Bell is another name that stands out in the archives at Queen's. Her mother Mary Shield had been at the College over twenty years before and had been a contemporary of Camilla Croudace, who, in 1883 when Gertrude arrived, was the Lady Resident. Gertrude Bell, who was to make her name as an Arabist, traveller, archaeologist, and diplomat, studied ancient history, English, French, German, scripture and arithmetic. In her letters home she complained of classes of thirty to forty girls and observed that 'the College is bitterly cold, one goes shivering from one class room to another'. But like many other bright girls who went on to make a name for themselves one particular teacher had a lasting influence on her. John de Soyres was a young Cambridge historian whom Gertrude greatly admired. 'He takes such broad views, never in the least one-sided, and he never says that is so but puts the two sides and tells one to choose. That's how history ought to be taught.'

During the 1850s and 1860s Queen's retained much of its founder's ideals. There was no corporal punishment, academic competition among the girls was discouraged and the rules about behaviour were more relaxed than at some of the other girls' schools. At North London Collegiate, for example, girls were taught a specially elegant way to descend the stairs. On the way down there was to be no talking. In class the girls could neither speak nor cough, and Miss Buss kept up a steady stream of do's and don'ts which many girls thought were irritating and unnecessary.

Girton College, Cambridge, founded by Emily Davies. It was started in Hitchin in 1869 and moved to Girton in 1873. Below: *Plaque in Girton College in honour of its founder.*

After Queen's spectacular beginning, the all-male management seemed to became fossilized in their success. Dorothea Beale, when she left the staff in 1856, felt that the main decision-making was too heavily concentrated in the office of the Principal and that the College needed more input from its women assistant tutors. There was also the question of the development of the College. There was, for instance, a reluctance to allow the girls to be examined by external examinations boards. As early as 1863 Emily Davies, a former student whose brother Llewelyn was later to become Principal of Queen's College, had successfully campaigned to get Cambridge University to hold a trial examination of girls at London day schools. Queen's entered some girls and again in the following year, but there was no enthusiasm for the concept of preparing girls for degree examinations. Emily Davies then applied for the post of assistant secretary at Queen's, hoping for a better opportunity to persuade the professors of the need for 'some plan for the affiliation of the College to the University of Cambridge'. Disheartened she turned her attention to the setting up of a new college for women at Hitchin in 1869 where a small group of students

SARAH EMILY DAVIES
Born April 22nd 1830
Died July 13th 1921 Aged 91
Throughout her life a leader in the struggle for the education and enfranchisement of women +++

By her faith and unwearied efforts this College was founded and established

Be strong & of a good courage

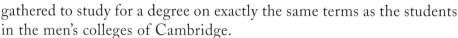

gathered to study for a degree on exactly the same terms as the students in the men's colleges of Cambridge.

In 1873 the students moved to the village of Girton on the outskirts of Cambridge and took the name Girton for the first of the all-women university colleges. The web of contacts and relationships spun at Queen's contributed to the establishment of Girton. Financial help came from Barbara Leigh Smith (later Mme Bodichon) who had attended some lectures at Queen's College, and who later successfully campaigned for the change in the law that enabled married women to have control of their property.

Another important Queen's connection was the erudite Lady Stanley of Alderly who helped to set up the Girls' Public Day School Company (later Trust). She was one of the influential Lady Visitors and a member of the Council at Queen's. She also gave Emily Davies her full support and at one stage took on the post of Mistress of Girton.

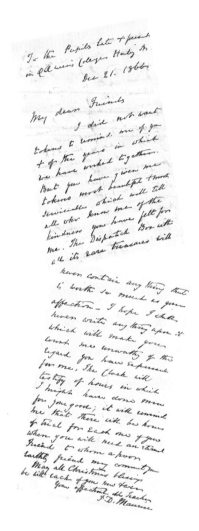

1874 was a year that tested the mettle of the College. The buildings started to collapse. The surveyor, hurriedly brought to Harley Street, found that 'a large portion of walls at the back of the house were in such a dangerous state that they could not be left as they were without great risk to the safety of the inmates and the pupils'. These houses, like so many of the buildings put up by speculative eighteenth-century builders in London, were not what they seemed. The Council of Queen's, appealing for emergency funds, declared 'as works proceeded, further defects showed themselves. The whole structure was found to have been built originally without any proper foundations, and of the worst possible materials.' The buildings were evacuated and temporary accommodation taken at 3 Stratford Place, just a block or two away, where the College carried on for six months while the buildings in Harley Street were repaired. Appealing to the public and its friends the Council of Queen's said that there were 200 pupils using the College every day and that repairs would cost a huge £50,000 – more than the College's entire reserves.

'It is proposed to give to all donors of 25 pounds and upwards, the right, during their life, of nominating one pupil in the College or School, at a reduction of three guineas per annum.' The more the donor subscribed the more children he could nominate until for £400 a scholarship could be founded, giving a free education in perpetuity.

Everyone rallied around – especially the staff. Once again, with Queen's in financial trouble, it is interesting to see how large a donation

Left: *The Waiting Room. Part of the plaster ceiling which survives today can be seen,* below. *The swirling design of an angel in flight has caught the attention of generations of girls. The plaster is thought to have been an original Adam design.*

Facing page: *F. D. Maurice and a letter he wrote to the School in 1866 thanking them for their gifts on the occasion of his departure for Cambridge to become Professor of Theology and Philosophy.*

individual professors were prepared to make. Several of them, including familiar names from the opening of the College like John Hullah and Thomas Astley Cock, gave £25 each. The Revd Plumptre found no less than £100 in the College's hour of need.

In the 1870s and 1880s Queen's suffered from the competition of the other London day schools. There was also a problem of clear decision-making in the College. There were three powerful groups, the Council, the Committee of Education, and the Lady Visitors, and disagreements among them were hard to resolve. Management was not helped by a remote Council that appointed the Principal who was invariably a clergyman-scholar. Two of the Principals went on to become Deans of Westminster – Stanley and Chenevix Trench.

Dean Plumptre, who served as Principal for two years at the end of a forty-year career at Queen's, resigned in 1877 and the new man, the Revd Llewelyn Davies, Emily's brother, tried to make sweeping changes. He envisaged a greatly expanded future for the College, offering education for girls from 8 years to 21. He wanted to introduce three stages, consisting

Mrs Alec Tweedie (Ethel Harley 1877–9), a distinguished Old Girl who produced a Jubilee Book for the College.

of the School, and a two-stage College providing three years of higher education ending in a degree given by Queen's and recognized by London University. The Council did not back the Principal and the scheme came to nothing. In 1882 the Council recorded in its minutes, 'It would be impossible for Queen's College, except by an outlay quite beyond its means, to compete with the ample provision of teaching thus offered to students who seek the BA degree.' No doubt the enormous cost of shoring up the crumbling buildings a few years before had taken its toll on the Council's confidence. At least some in the College community objected enough to see that a poem called 'University Rhyme' appeared in the November issue of the *College Magazine*:

> BA, BA, black gowns
> Have you a degree?
> Yes Miss, that I have, one, two, three.
> One for Bedford College, and one for Cheltenham,
> But none for the girls at Queen's,
> Whom no one now will cram.
>
> Little bluestocking, come blow me your horn,
> The girls go to Girton and Queen's is forlorn.
> Where is the Professor who looks after the sheep?
> Snug in his armchair fast asleep.

Bedford College, founded one year after Queen's, took a different course. It did not give up the struggle to prepare girls for university degrees. Perhaps it was the tenacity of a woman Principal, combined with a government grant, neither of which Queen's had, that kept Bedford going forward towards a closer relationship with London University. By 1900 half of the students were preparing for graduation and Bedford had become a college of the University.

Queen's celebrated its Golden Jubilee in 1898 with a ball, a production of Shakespeare's *Twelfth Night*, a special church service, and a series of lectures. A Jubilee Book was compiled by Mrs Alec Tweedie, who had been at Queen's twenty years before. Old girls wrote about their memories of the College and gave a précis of their career. Some like Mrs Tweedie, who had won fame as a traveller, painter and writer, had been destined to become society hostesses. Others recorded their experiences as women who had made it in a man's world. Maud Beerbohm Tree, the actress wife of the celebrated nineteenth-century actor-manager, wrote a lyrical gushing account of the College that any modern 'luvvie' would have envied. There were girls who had become hospital matrons, workhouse superintendents, missionaries, and one, Frederica Fleay, wrote about being the managing director and chairman of a brewery.

But the Jubilee's great moment came when Queen Victoria sent word that she would call at the College on 9 May 1898. In the words of Dorothy Burr, who was at the school from 1897 to 1903:

> One bright morning we were all told to return home, put on our white dresses and come back in the afternoon, when we were all lined up on the pavement outside the College. A rumour went round that the Queen is coming. Presently a carriage and pair appeared – in it was seated the wonderful little figure, all in black, of Queen Victoria.

The Queen's own account of the visit is in the Royal Archives at Windsor:

> After breakfast left for London. It was rather dull, but there were a great many people out, driving from Paddington. Took half an hour's turn in the garden, after reaching the Palace. After luncheon I received the Chilean Minister and saw Lord Salisbury who looked and seemed well, but the war between Spain and the United States was of course a great source of anxiety. The thought of the dear Queen Regent makes one so anxious and unhappy. The African difficulty with France Lord Salisbury hopes looks much better. Drove with Beatrice and

Above: *Detail from a painting, by drawing teacher Ella Bedford, of Queen Victoria's visit for the College's Golden Jubilee on 9 May 1898. The Queen is being presented with a bouquet by the Queen's Scholar Kathleen Croudace, niece of the Lady Resident.*

Left: *An extract from the Queen's diary, written in the hand of her daughter Beatrice, who copied the diary before it was destroyed on the Queen's instructions.*

71

Annie R. On my way out stopped at Queen's College in Harley Street, the first Ladies College ever founded in England, which is this year celebrating its Jubilee. All the girls and ladies were drawn up outside. The Principal [Dr Robinson] the Dean [Professor Seely] and Mrs Robinson were presented to me. The Principal handed [me] an address, and Miss Croudace, the Queen's scholar for the year, a beautiful basket of roses. Drove afterwards by the Marble Arch into the Park. Took tea on coming home.

Historian Elaine Kaye summed up the position of Queen's at the turn of

The cast of the production of Twelfth Night, *one of the events marking the College's Golden Jubilee.* Back row, left to right: *Blanche Read (Sir Toby Belch), Sylvia Jones (Malvolio), Miss Debenham (Maria), Irene Cross (Fabian), H. Gardner (Valentine), G. Butler (Duke's attendant), S. Dalrymple (Viola), Dorothy Kendal Grimston (Count Orsino);* front row, left to right: *Rose Corfield (Clown), Mabel Davis (Olivia), Nola Kerin (Sebastian), Dorothy McKenna (Curio).*

the century just over fifty years since the governesses and the professors made their historic leap into further education for women:

> Queen's was not destined to become a college of any university, although the idea of amalgamating with an existing college of London University was suggested several times before 1914. The practice of giving 'higher' lectures, and lectures for the general public, refused to die. By 1900 the College had established a tradition of a broad and liberal education, preparing some for further study at university, and giving others a final preparation for entry into professional and domestic life. At the time of the Jubilee, the College 'could look back on fifty years' achievement'; fifty years in which the whole position of women in society had changed.

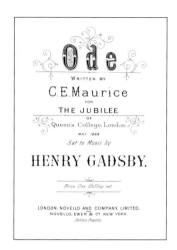

A song was specially composed for the Golden Jubilee by the history professor C. E. Maurice.

Professor Henry Gadsby, Harmony and Vocal Music, 1882–1907.

Founder's Day Service at Westminster Abbey, 28 March 1928.

CHAPTER SIX

'YOUR COUNTRY NEEDS YOU'

THE NEW CENTURY STARTED WITH GREAT EXCITEMENT at Queen's. Londoners followed Britain's changing fortunes in the Boer War. When Ladysmith was relieved, and later when Mafeking, a small railway town which had been under siege by the Boers for 217 days, was also relieved, the girls at Queen's reacted in a frenzy of excited celebration.

Evelyn Payne's diary of 1900, written when she was a First Junior, and one of the treasures of the Queen's College archives, captures the heady spirit of the girls as the battles with the Boers progressed. Evelyn described how their physical exercise class turned into war games when they heard that British forces under Dundonald had entered Ladysmith:

> We had a splendid patriotic drill. Miss Croudace, Harper, etc., all attended. First we marched around with Union Jacks singing 'God Save the Queen'. Then we gave three cheers for Dundonald (as his niece was here). Then we exercised with flags and charging drill. Afterwards we sang the 'Absent Minded Beggar' and gave three cheers for General Buller as a wind up. At drawing we heard the orchestra class sing 'God Save the Queen' and the old fool of a Mr Bedford (art professor) actually grumbled 'What are ye all so patriotic about today?' I could have kicked him.

The C. Company of the Royal Canadian Regiment, seizing a 'kopje' during the Boer War.

75

The days dragged by as Evelyn, and all her early teenage friends at Queen's, waited for news. In her diary on Friday, 18 May 1900 she noted that everyone was waiting breathlessly. 'The air is so still it feels that something was going to happen.' Evelyn, who lived at 78 Wimpole Street, just around the corner from Queen's, eventually had to go to bed:

> I was lying in bed reading *Henry V* and rejoicing in its patriotic spirit of glory of England in war when about 10.30 p.m. I heard cheers which gradually increased . . . everyone was standing at their front doors . . . we heard shouts of 'Mafeking relieved' and I only hoped it was true. The cheers when I was back in bed were tremendous. Increasingly one could hear the sound echoing in all directions as if the whole of London was shouting.

Evelyn's diary goes on to describe a bus ride through London to the City and the crush of people around the Mansion House. Her account recalls how she went to the house of the hero of Mafeking, Col. Robert Baden-Powell, near Marble Arch. 'Here was a charming scene, the drive and road in front packed

Funeral procession of Queen Victoria, 1901 (below), *and* (above) *part of the Royal patronage book showing donations to various schools including Queen's College.*

with people who joined in cheering – for every bus that passed stopped and all the people stood up with their hats off as if for the Queen, and cheered.'

A more sober and saddened London mourned the death of Queen Victoria in January 1901. The girls wore black armbands and recalled that the Queen had supported the College for more than half a century. In the patronage book at the Royal Archives in Windsor Castle the entries show how the Queen gave donations to Queen's College and other schools. Names, dates, and amounts are all sedately listed in a clerk's copperplate hand. The patronage book also records the names of 'Queen's College Scholars' students whose fees were paid by Queen Victoria. Camilla Croudace's niece, Kathleen, happened to be one of the recipients in 1897!

The College had become settled and comfortable in its role of offering middle- and upper-class girls a comprehensive and unique education. Some aristocratic families also chose to send their daughters. It had not changed much in its ethos. It still opened some of its lectures to the general public, an activity that is echoed in the Thursday lectures today, when, along with the girls, there are sometimes parents and friends in the audience. Curiously, for an institution that nurtured girls who were destined to reform education and fight for women's rights, Queen's was still run by clergymen and professors. Many of the nineteenth-century cast of teachers and professors were still there, with two and sometimes three generations of students behind them. Such a system, with so many male teachers on the staff, looked very outdated alongside other girls' schools of the day. Camilla Croudace, elderly and stately, carried on as Lady Resident. She had come to Queen's in 1881 having been a much-travelled governess and schoolteacher. She had also been a student at Queen's in the 1850s. 'She always wore a becoming lace cap,' recalled one of her students at the beginning of the century, 'which for special occasions was of Honiton Lace' (a textile much favoured by Queen Victoria herself). There was more than a touch of the society hostess about her. Well connected socially, she had a suite of rooms above the College in Harley Street where she was fond of giving parties to which the girls would be invited. There is a reference in a girl's diary at the turn of the century about Miss Croudace's cottage at Haslemere in Surrey where she would often invite senior students for the weekend. Indeed it was said of her that she excelled at giving the girls those social graces that made it possible for many of them to become wives of ambassadors.

The woman who taught French, Mademoiselle Marie Séguin, had been at Queen's since 1879, teaching for a few hours a week. She wore

Camilla Croudace, Lady Resident from 1881 to 1906. A former pupil, she was respected and admired by those under her care.

Clara Wood, the doyenne of the boarding house at Queen's. Students remembered her dressed in shades of purple and lavender and wearing a velvet ribbon bow round her head.

layers of clothes, a veritable walking wardrobe, which she hoped would protect her from any germs. She was fixated on the possibility of getting a cold in the head and closed all the windows to keep the germs at bay. Anyone who threatened her health by bringing out a handkerchief was instantly told 'Dolly, Dolly' (she called all the girls Dolly) 'handkerchiefs in pockets'. She told the girls that she had spent her youth during the siege of Paris eating rats and that 'men's beards were used in the making of bread'. No wonder the girls liked her, despite her habit of returning exercise books by throwing them across the classroom.

Queen's records confirm that she had a delicate constitution and that the doctors 'forbad her to go from room to room', so it was arranged that she had a room of her own and that all the pupils would go to her. In the holidays Mlle Séguin was often a house guest of families whose girls she taught, a list that one might find in *Who's Who* today: Lady Folkeston, the Countess of Radnor, Lady Balfour, Lady Lothian, Sir Henry Craik, and Lord Salisbury. In 1911 she had a row with the Council of Queen's over pay and resigned. When she died at the age of 82 and her will was printed in the paper, old Queen's girls were agog. Careful with her money, she gave the impression of living a frugal life with few luxuries in a small flat in Marylebone. But she left the huge amount of £18,000 to various church charities. Gwendoline Holloway, the first woman Principal of Queen's, commented, 'I had no idea she was as wealthy as that for she lived very simply. She was an amazingly good teacher and very full of life. I believe that she retired when fees for teaching were even less than they are now but she might have had private pupils.'

At the turn of the century students were either day girls, doing a structured course of lectures for an annual fee, or 'non-compounders', attending lectures on an *ad hoc* basis. There were also girls at the College and the School who boarded. There had been boarding houses right from the start, as, in the 1850s, several people in the area of Queen's offered to provide board and lodging. 'Mrs Dovers, 69 Wimpole Street receives pupils of the College into her house for board and maternal superintendence: Terms – 40 guineas per annum.'

Clara Wood was the doyenne of the boarding house business. She leased number 41 Harley Street, and the upper part of 43, and students remembered her dressed in shades of purple and lavender. She wore a velvet ribbon round her head with a bow to match the dress. Fond of going to Covent Garden, she bustled along with purple sequins flashing in the lamplight. 'At 9 o'clock, we left our preparation or practising and strolled into the Waiting Room where Miss Wood presided over tea and biscuits in which "squashed flies" figured largely. She told stories about the professors which gave a human side to them.'

There were musical evenings in the Waiting Room and dances in the Pfeiffer Hall – not a male partner in sight, of course, except for an intrepid professor or two. The boarders played tennis in Regent's Park and hockey and netball at Maida Vale. There were various societies including the Swanwick Society at which girls and members of the staff would read poetry and discuss literary subjects. There were evenings to which parents and friends were invited such as the one on Wednesday, 27 November 1900 which Evelyn Payne and her family attended:

> There were crowds of people [she wrote] and a mixture of evening dress and hats . . . We saw Mr Hall-Griffin beforehand – he looked so nice and handsome in evening dress – twice as nice as in class. The evening opened with a short address in broken English by Signor Ricci (he seems such a nice man and is most popular with his pupils). Then Hall-Griffin began. His voice trembled, but as he warmed to it he became absolutely in his element. He is a perfectly passionate Browning enthusiast and like an inspired man on his theme. It was splendid. The lecture was illustrated by magnificent slides from photos taken himself of every place mentioned in the poem – one continuous stream of glorious views – and the torrent of eloquence that accompanied them in his own excited language of long extracts read in a deep trembling thrilling voice. I couldn't believe it was the same man who taught us and made vulgar jokes in a nasal voice.

Evelyn's diary of 1900 is full of such graphic descriptions of life at Queen's. Her father, Frank, was a physician and Queen's was just around the corner from his consulting rooms in Wimpole Street. He was one of those unusual Victorian fathers who believed passionately in women's education. Evelyn's diary, meticulously kept for most of 1900, captures the quality of middle-class family life as well as the highlights of the British army's progress through Africa. The printed pages in the front of the diary give all sorts of useful information for a 'first junior' at Queen's: the start of the partridge-shooting season, John Locke's date of birth, the founding of the British Museum, eclipses of the sun and the moon, lists of all the army regiments, and the information 'that passports are not required, the

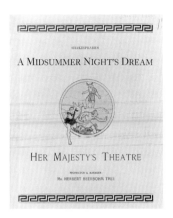

The programme for A Midsummer Night's Dream, *attended by some Queen's pupils.*

rule having been virtually relaxed, for travellers who visit the countries of France, Belgium, Spain, Denmark, Sweden, Norway, Italy or Holland'. Evelyn stuck programmes of favourite concerts in the front and the back of the diary along with clippings from newspapers with quotations from Keats and Shakespeare. The diary tells us of the intense social life that the girls at Queen's enjoyed, including tea parties at each other's houses, some with professional entertainers on special occasions; visits to the theatre to see *A Midsummer Night's Dream* in which Mrs Beerbohm Tree, a former pupil, was starring. *Jack and the Beanstalk* was the Christmas treat. Several afternoons or evenings she went with friends or the family to hear recitals in concert halls. Evelyn's nurse or her mother took her for walks in Hyde Park and Regent's Park, and on expeditions with bags of whitebait to feed the gulls in St James's Park. The family went away to the country or the seaside for term holidays and during the summer of 1900 the family took a house in the Lake District.

Evelyn gives the impression of a warm and harmonious relationship with her parents, despite a certain formality, '25 January: had breakfast with Mother and Father for first time. I am going to give up nursery breakfast forever now!' Her parents were interested in art and occasionally the diary reveals a hint of the parents' social life. 'Friday 16 Feb: had horrid Latin. I do hate it, French conversation. Did a picture and talked about going to the dentist. A great French painter M. Monet – came to dinner (he can speak no English).' But the centre of Evelyn's world was undoubtedly Queen's. She reveals a warmth about the way the staff dealt with the girls and their sensitive egos, and the perennial problem of homework:

> Wednesday 14: I had such a headache last night that my theology was excused. Mr Sharpe [theology teacher] was horrified and seemed to think that I was lazy. My friend 'Do' told Miss L [Miss Luard, head of the School] about it, who came round at dinner time and kissed me on the top of my head and said he did not know Evelyn.

In 1911 the College took a house in St John's Wood to be used as sick quarters for the boarding houses. Two rooms at the top of the house were kept free for any emergencies and the woman of the house was paid to clean, cook and nurse the patients. It was, however, a short-lived outstation of the College. The Council decided in 1914 to end the arrangement and take out a subscription at the London Fever Hospital in Liverpool Road, North London. They were promised sympathetic treatment should a patient be sent from the College, and if possible a private room.

At weekends the boarders visited galleries and museums, and were taken to concerts on Saturday afternoons. They walked in crocodiles all over London and got up to mischief when they could. Beryl Dollar, *née* Lockwood (1918–29), got the better of at least one teacher: 'One success we had was on the dreaded "early walk", 8.15–8.50 a.m. We walked past my mother's house and turned in – we were given a second breakfast and sent back to school by car. We were not missed.' Beryl and her sister Joy should have been at St Trinian's, not Queen's. 'Joy, my sister, was expelled. It was put more graciously than that, but she turned a seven-pound jar of malt on its side and watched it trickle down the staircase outside Matron's office. Another time she locked Miss Beatrice Baird (head of the boarders) in her bedroom and threw the key into Harley Street.' But those boarders who stayed the course and got their certificates, girls like Kathleen Bainbridge-Bell (1909–12), felt that they knew every corner of the West End:

Queen's College boarders on an outing in Regent's Park. Katherine Mansfield appears second from left in the back row.

Once when a newly arrived and unsophisticated foreign teacher was in charge, the leaders took us to the Burlington Arcade where we spent

The Beauchamp family at Las Palmas on their way to England in 1903. Standing left to right: Katherine Mansfield, Harold Beauchamp, Ship's Officer Crow, Uncle Dyer, Vera Beauchamp. Sitting left to right: 'Chaddie' Beauchamp, Mrs Beauchamp, Leslie Beauchamp, Captain Fishwick, Jeanne Beauchamp and Belle Dyer.

a pleasant time shop-gazing. Some one innocently referred to this at dinner and caused a tremendous sensation; I was left with the idea that some undefined evil haunted the place, and sought out a monitor afterwards and asked if this was merely Miss Wood's imagination, but was mysteriously informed that it was true. She or someone else told me later that the Burlington Arcade could be visited with impunity before 11 o'clock in the morning.

The cosy-sounding routine of the boarding house was soon to be shaken by the arrival in 1903 of a young girl of 14 from New Zealand, who was to become one of the great literary figures of the twentieth century. Katherine Mansfield – her real name was Beauchamp – came from a wealthy colonial family in Wellington. Her father, Harold Beauchamp, had made a comfortable fortune in business and banking, and, fond of adventure and travel himself, decided to send Katherine and her two sisters to Queen's. Beauchamp cousins, Sylvia and Evelyn Payne, the diarist whose parents lived in Wimpole Street, were already at Queen's. Katherine joined them, thrilled at loosening the shackles of genteel colonial life. Unlike her schools in New Zealand, Queen's College was remark-

Facing page: *One of Katherine Mansfield's short stories from the* Queen's College Magazine, *December 1903.*

ably relaxed and had not succumbed to excessive rule-making and a rigid school uniform. As Katherine Mansfield's biographer, Claire Tomalin, describes, even the curriculum was amazingly flexible:

> From Katherine's records it is clear that girls were allowed to concentrate on favourite subjects and drop others altogether. She soon gave up theology, chemistry, geography, ancient history, drawing and arithmetic (for which she received 0 out of 150 in a scholarship paper) and kept only German, French, English, singing and 'cello. A minimum of ten hours a week in class was expected with an hour of private study in preparation for each class.

She and her sisters shared an attic room which looked out over the roofs of London, and her letters read like a eulogy for her school. 'I lived in the girls, the professors, the big lovely building, the leaping fires in winter and the abundant flowers in summer.'

Katherine enthusiastically joined the debating society, played the 'cello and, while writing short stories for the school magazine, decided on her famous *nom de plume* – her own second name. She became the editor of the magazine. Her journal gives many insights into life at Queen's in the first four years of the twentieth century. She was apparently disappointed that she never learnt French from Monsieur Huguenot:

> What an opportunity missed! What has it not cost me! He lectured in a big narrow room that was painted all over – the walls, door, and window-frames – a grey shade of mignonette green. The ceiling was white, and just below it there was a frieze of long looped chains of white flowers. On either side of the marble mantlepiece a naked small boy staggered under a big platter of grapes that he held above his head. Below the windows, far below, there was a stable court paved in cobble stones, and one could hear the faint clatter of carriages coming out or in, the noise of water gushing out of a pump into a big pail – some youth clumping about and whistling.

Comments from her contemporaries and teachers tell us that Katherine was not a popular girl. She was moody and possessive. Claire Tomalin records what contemporaries said of one of her friends, a girl called Vere Bartrick-Baker: 'the two girls would meet in the school's dark lower corridor before lessons began, to discuss the ideas of their favourite writers,

and were apparently suspected of "immorality" of a kind unspecified'.

Katherine Mansfield's most lasting friendship was also made at Queen's, with Ida Baker, someone she would know all her life.

> The first day she noticed Katherine's dark eyes observing everything about her. Then she found they shared a taste for poetry. Later, walking in Regent's Park, Katherine turned to her and asked commandingly, 'Shall we be friends?' Almost from that moment, Ida saw herself as devoted to Katherine's service; she would spend hours sitting with her in her room, listening as she practised her 'cello or talking about Katherine's plans, Katherine's future, Katherine's life. To Ida, Katherine seemed extraordinary in her dark beauty and her intensity.

There can be no doubt about the influence of the teachers at Queen's on the young tempestuous and rebellious Katherine. One was Richard

Katherine Mansfield
(right) *in 1906,*
(above) *in 1921.*

Gregory, Professor of Astronomy from 1897 to 1918, who taught at Queen's before being appointed Astronomer Royal. The young Professor Walter Rippmann, her German teacher, also inspired her to read the works of Oscar Wilde, Tolstoy, Ibsen, and Bernard Shaw. In a letter to her cousin Sylvia Payne she wrote: 'I am ashamed at the way in which I long for German, I simply can't help it. It is dreadful and when I go into class I feel I must stare at him all the time.'

After three years the Beauchamps took Katherine back to New Zealand but the Antipodes could hold her frustrated energy for only two years. In 1908 she was back in London to begin a career that was both brilliantly productive but personally erratic and tragic. During a whirlwind of lesbian and heterosexual relationships she became pregnant, and married a man who was not the father – all within two years. Her medical records investigated by Claire Tomalin revealed that she suffered from what appears to be the symptoms of gonorrhoea – arthritis, heart trouble, and pleurisy. She had become a chronic invalid by 1910 with much of her best work still to come.

Sylvia Pankhurst, daughter of Emmeline Pankhurst, addresses a crowd in Bow Road, London, 1912, as part of the 'Votes for Women' campaign.

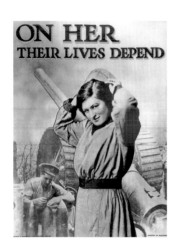

ON HER
THEIR LIVES DEPEND

The role women played as part of the war effort proved their ability to do traditionally male jobs and helped to change fundamentally their role in the post-war society.

Her face was often described as being like a mask. She was pale and dark, innocent and decadent, first too fat and then too thin. She was sexually ambiguous, with a husband and a wife, and lovers of both sexes. In her lifetime she was disliked both as a person and as a writer, and also revered as both. Not many people took a stance between these two attitudes, although some like Virginia Woolf and D. H. Lawrence alternated. The testimony left by these two friends, each outstandingly gifted and sensitive to other people, is of the greatest importance in trying to understand Katherine. She herself cared a great deal for friendship. Her letters went out in convoys, seeking reassurance and making offerings; but she was also manipulative and treacherous. The letters and journals are dizzying switchbacks of love and hate as well as vivid records of work, travel and suffering.

Queen's had a good war. No bombs dropped out of the sky to wreck Harley Street. Girls continued to come and go every day. There was no question of evacuation and the boarding house maintained its numbers with about twenty girls. The danger from the sky did alarm people after May 1915 when a Zeppelin dropped an incendiary bomb over East London killing six and injuring thirty-five. From then on policemen bicycled around the streets carrying signs that read 'Take cover'. Maroon rockets were also fired if German aircraft appeared and the staff at Queen's had an arrangement with a parent who lived in Blackheath in south-east London to telephone the College if she saw a German aeroplane or Zeppelin coming over. The girls then scuttled down into the basement with blankets and hot drinks until either a policeman or a Boy Scout with a bugle sounded the 'All Clear' in Harley Street.

At Queen's some of the girls wrote letters to two prisoners of war who had been adopted by the College and parcels were made up and dispatched. The College records show how the Old Girls also became deeply involved in the war effort. 'Greenhalgh has gone to France as an ambulance motor driver; Annie and Catherine Hill have gone to Château d'Oex to see their brother who is a prisoner there; B. Hutchinson, First Aid Nursing in France; D. James and J. Hamilton making aeroplane parts at White City.' Many more Old Girls had joined government ministries and local government organizations to help with the war effort and many are listed as working in hospitals.

An important innovation that was made during the war years concerned examination by outside educational bodies. The new Principal,

Professor Kendall, who took over from Sir Henry Craik in 1915, instigated examinations of all First Senior students by the Oxford Senior Local examination. It was also agreed, despite the traditional Queen's suspicion of outside interference and academic competition, that all Second Senior students should be encouraged to take the Oxford Higher Local examination. Professor Kendall also started the College day at 9.30 a.m. instead of 10 a.m. and made the terms one week longer.

When the bells rang out the Armistice in November 1918 the pubs stayed open until they were dry and a war-weary nation had to come to terms with the loss of a generation of men and boys. Throughout Europe there was a shocking toll of 9 million killed and about 17 million wounded.

The College, pictured soon after the First World War.

Queen's had to begin to react to a new post-war society in which women, who could make aeroplane parts and drive ambulances, aspired to play a larger role in commerce and government. In 1919 a new secretarial department was added to the College. There had already been a controversial move to teach domestic science as early as 1901 and training girls to type must have been perceived by some as another step away from higher education. Academic sensibilities, however, would have been somewhat soothed by the structure of the course: English, History, and at least one modern language, along with secretarial studies, in order to obtain a College certificate. The take-up of these courses under the remarkable Miss L. M. Dean, a teacher who spanned generations of girls and died in office in 1964, was encouraging enough for the Council to think about expansion. The lease of 47 Harley Street, still the property of the GBI, came up for sale and after an appeal fund raised £10,000 the lease was bought, and, following alterations, the building was ready for use in 1925. More space was therefore available for the Domestic Science department which taught post-war young women how to manage cooking and domestic arrangements with fewer servants.

A reporter from the *Evening News* wrote that the girls were first sent out shopping and judged on what they bought when they returned to the College. The Principal Professor Joseph Edwards explained, 'We all try our best to produce a more efficient housewife of the future, giving the girls a chance to learn the real things they will need.' Presumably the Professor's comments about academic achievements were cut by the paper's sub-editor. Crucially, however, the girls' culinary prowess was often judged by Lady Visitors who came to lunch.

The acquisition of 47 Harley Street also gave the College the room that is most warmly remembered by the Old Girls and staff, the existing main library on the first floor overlooking Harley Street. Students helped to carry the books to the new site stacked in laundry baskets. In 1928 Queen Mary visited the College and saw a new block of classrooms and the gymnasium that replaced a number of shops and small artisans' houses in the mews at the back of Harley Street. Queen Mary's visit was written up in the magazine. 'Her Majesty had tea in the library and was afterwards conducted to the hall where Stephanie Tyacke, the youngest girl in the hostel, presented her with a bouquet.'

That little 9-year-old from Cornwall grew up to become one of the legendary Principals of Queen's. She said that as the youngest girl in the School, she was 'caught, cleaned up and corralled, and spent the rest of the day practising to curtsey in front of Miss Holloway with a hand full of paper as a bouquet'. Stephanie Fierz (Principal 1964–83) remembers every detail of her first arrival. She was delivered to Harley Street, as arranged, the day before term began but the place was locked up. The School had forgotten that she was coming that evening. Next day her mother brought her back and a lifelong relationship with Queen's began. As the youngest boarder in the School, she remembers being treated very kindly by everyone:

> My bed was in room 12. I had a cubicle in a room divided into four by bars with curtains on them. My cubicle was on the right as you came in the door and in it was a wardrobe, a bed, a wash stand with a jug and basin etc., a chest of drawers with a looking-glass on it, a chair and a laundry basket. My trunk was unpacked in the Hall of 47 Harley

Revd Canon G. C. Bell, Principal 1904–10.

Sir Henry Craik, Principal 1911–15 (left); Professor Joseph Edwards, Principal 1919–31 (right).

Street by the Matron and I carried the stuff upstairs to my cubicle. The trunks were then taken downstairs to the basement of 47 to be stored until the end of term.

Above left: *Chemistry lesson, c.1920s, in what was probably the first chemistry laboratory in a girls' school. The teacher is Professor Ellis Richards;* above right: *a Boarders' dormitory room, c.1930s.*

Her mother, a fun-loving widow who managed to spend whatever capital came her way, decided to send Stephanie to Queen's because 'she decided I seemed to be so plain that I would never attract a man to keep me in the state she had taught me to expect'. Stephanie, said her mother, must go to university and have a career but under no circumstances become an unqualified governess. Mrs Fierz remembers washing her hair and drying it in front of the fire on every other Friday. The maids would wake the girls in the morning with hot cans of water and again at the end of the day another can would be brought up so that the girls could wash and change for dinner. The evening meal, a formal occasion, was taken in the Waiting Room. There was always a member of staff at the head of each table; white tablecloths and maids to serve the food. 'The food was very good,' she recalled, 'usually three courses with a lovely pudding of some kind.' After dinner there were prayers in the library taken by the Lady Resident who would also take the youngest ones to her room and read to them before they went to bed.

The food was always a bit special on Saturday nights. They would have chicken as a special treat and strawberries and cream. Afterwards there would be a party, 'and we would dance with each other to gramophone records and play charades, and end the evening with lemonade and chocolate biscuits'. Church on Sundays was at the Abbey. They would go by bus and have the privilege of sitting in the choir stalls. The two

MISS. PEGGY SALAMAN with JUBA & JOKA
The two lion cubs were found in Africa by Miss Salaman, who with Mr Gordon Store in Nov. 1931 set up a record of 5 days, 6 hrs, 40 mins. for the flight from England to Cape Town in an all British "Puss Moth" aeroplane.

Two remarkable Old Girl aviators.

This page: *Peggy Salaman, who broke the London to Cape Town light aeroplane record in the Kings Cup air race of October 1931. She took five days, six hours and 40 minutes in her single-engined De Havilland Puss Moth, and picked up the two lion cubs en route to South Africa.*

Facing page: *Diana Barnato Walker in the cockpit of a taxi-Anson. On 26 August 1963 she became the first British woman to fly through the sound barrier (1,262 mph) in a two-seat training version of the Lightning (XM996) aircraft. Inset: In her débutante's dress, 1936. (Picture by Norman Parkinson.)*

Principals of Queen's who had gone on to become Deans of Westminster had kept their links with the College. Mrs Fierz remembers that there was always a maid in uniform at the front door of 43 Harley Street to make sure that the young ladies put their gloves on before stepping out into Harley Street. The boarders (there were only about twenty) were well occupied at weekends going ice skating at Bayswater, to the theatre in the West End, and on outings to the country. Stephanie even went hacking in Hyde Park. The school arranged for a horse to be brought around to the College and she would mount from the pavement. 'Goodness only knows what it cost, anyway I don't think my mother ever paid the bill. She was always behind with the fees and years later when I became a teacher at Queen's College, there were still outstanding fees, which I settled.' Mrs Fierz's mother was not the only one to forget the fees. When she was Principal in the late 1960s Mrs Fierz received a letter with a cheque. It was from a parent whose daughter was at Queen's in the 1920s saying that she had always been ashamed at not paying the fees and was now putting the matter right – almost thirty years later!

The type of girl that Queen's attracted had not changed much since Evelyn Payne's day: a lot of doctors' daughters from near by and a smattering of aristocratic girls in the boarding house. The day girls were still brought to Harley Street by nannies and nurses. One of the girls,

Stephanie Fierz remembers, was Unity Mitford, one of Lord Redesdale's daughters, who became notorious for her visits to Germany as the guest of Hitler before the Second World War. At Queen's, according to Mrs Fierz, she was a talented artist, and very naughty. 'She used to draw cruel caricatures of teachers and leave them around for the staff to see.' One victim, when given news of Unity's 'coming out' (launched into London society at a débutantes' ball) was heard to remark, 'I don't care where she's gone so long as she's left here.'

A significant number of girls left at 16, to take part in the round of balls and parties that ended in the débutantes' presentation at Buckingham Palace. Another contemporary of Stephanie Fierz in the 1930s was Diana Barnato Walker, the granddaughter of the South African diamond magnate, Barney Barnato, the co-founder of the De Beers diamond-mining company. Diana lived with her mother in Primrose Hill and sometimes visited her father, Wolf Barnato, at the Brooklands racing track at weekends. She would arrive back at school brimming over with stories of her father's Le Mans racing Bentleys (he became chairman of Bentley Motors) and how she had been allowed to go around the circuit with him. Stephanie went to Diana's débutante ball at the Dorchester and found her very disappointed. She had expected to be presented to King Edward VIII

Classroom activities in the 1930s.

Left and right: *Needlework and dress-making.*
Below: *Domestic science in what is now the Bovell-Sturge Science Laboratory (rebuilt in 1985).*

at the garden party that afternoon, but after meeting a long line of curt-seying beauties, the King got fed up and walked away. Perhaps it was the thrill of high speed that led Diana into commercial flying and to become the first British woman to fly a jet through the sound barrier. She remembers that at College the girls just wore what they wished. But there were rules about what they could wear to games outside the school: navy-blue gym tunic and white blouse. There were also green and silver hat bands with the College crest, plain green ties for the School, and green and silver ties for the College and a blazer.

Maria Xenia Cawadias, the daughter of a Greek doctor who lived at 52 Wimpole Street, was sent to Queen's after the family settled in London in the mid-1920s. 'The best children's shop in those early pre-war days was Daniel Neal's in Portman Square, and, since nanny Nell always insisted on the best, she and my mother took me there to be fitted out. I tried on shirts, ties, lace-up shoes, a gym tunic and a blazer with a large green and silver badge and a black velour hat.' In her biography, *Xenia – A Memoir of Greece 1919–1949*, written after a career as war correspondent during the Greek Civil War, Maria Henderson (she married

Right: *Gym.*
Below: *The teacher poses for the girls'*
art class in the old art room (left);
Chemistry with Mrs LeFevre (right).

the distinguished British diplomat Sir Nicholas Henderson) described the house in Wimpole Street as tall and narrow with two or three rooms on each floor. 'There were open fires throughout the house and elegant marble Adam fireplaces, lots of stairs, and coils of shiny banisters which I could slide down when Nell was not looking. A staff of ten was engaged by Nell, headed by a butler. The hierarchy descended right down to the Irish kitchen maid who was always giving in her notice.'

In her early years at Queen's Maria was very sensitive about being foreign. Her features were Mediterranean and she was physically more developed than most of the English girls in her class. She confesses to kicking over the traces just to test the rules and, having spoken French for years in Greece, had a maddening habit of correcting the French teacher's pronunciation (she called it a French accident not an accent),

but in spite of all this I enjoyed school and made a number of good friends. We used to sit together – usually on the radiators to keep warm in the winter – giggling and discussing life (I seemed to get worse chilblains than they did – school was incredibly cold but this was considered healthy) I came to like many of my teachers too – with the exception of the games and gym teachers. And I loved the new world they led me into: the world of books and poetry, Bacon, Milton, Keats, Wordsworth, and Shelley, had become part of my private conversations with myself.

During the late 1920s, the professors' grip on the management of the College began to loosen. No doubt they realized that the College was looking antediluvian in its management alongside the new high schools and the ladies' colleges and that a nod in the direction of the twentieth century was well overdue. They made a modest start in 1926 by appointing Miss Gwendoline Holloway as the Senior Tutor, and two years later she was formally appointed as Headmistress of the School and Vice-Principal of the College. The Principal, Professor Edwards, while being considered 'adorable' by everyone, had allowed the running of the College to become a bit lax. Miss Holloway, when she was appointed Principal in 1932, made many innovations including the introduction of elected prefects and a new modern studies course. She encouraged girls to go to university. Joann Healey (Joann Puttick 1932–9) remembers her well, she had a kind face and an interest in the arts:

> We were in awe of her. She could be very strict. Once when a teacher was driven crazy by talking in class, she sent the whole form to the Principal's office. One by one we had to go in to be sternly reprimanded by Miss Holloway and to recite a poem, that we had learned by heart, in front of her. It had the right effect, we did not talk again in class, but what a long procedure.

Miss Holloway, according to Stephanie Fierz, was a very good judge of people and astute at hiring teachers. 'She brought the College into modern times, appointed an excellent staff and left them alone to get on with it.' Joann Healey remembers that she had a beautiful reading voice and that she took morning prayers with great dignity. The verses from the Bible read at prayers gave her a deep appreciation of the language of the King James Bible which she has never forgotten. Miss Holloway was human enough to blush, to the great amusement of the girls. 'It happened, only once, at Annual Gathering when the Bishop commented on the Principal's beautiful speaking voice. She went pink from the neck up.' The

A policeman warns of an air raid in 1939. Displaying a sign reading 'Take Cover' was a practice carried over from the First World War.

new better-qualified members of staff that replaced the lacklustre group Miss Holloway inherited, made a big difference to the academic standard at the time. Mrs Ethel Truman, the first woman to get a first in physics at London University, was one of Holloway's appointments, an excellent teacher with a modern approach to science who guided many Queen's girls, including Stephanie Fierz, towards science degrees. Mrs Truman taught at Queen's until her retirement in 1968.

It fell to Miss Holloway to deal with the crisis that faced all London schools as the political situation in Europe deteriorated in the late 1930s. The girls kept a log of all that happened during the autumn of 1938.

Prime Minister Neville Chamberlain announces 'Peace in our time', 1938. Below: Letter of acknowledgement from the Prime Minister to the School.

> There was an unbearable feeling of tension everywhere. It was impossible to concentrate on ordinary work. People went about their business with grave and anxious faces. There were frenzied ARP preparations: gas-masks were delivered and fitted; the digging of trenches went on day and night in parks and squares; rooms were made gasproof; hospitals and public buildings were sandbagged . . . and arrangements were made for thousands of children to be evacuated.

Queen's had booked a guest house in the Lake District and in late September 1938 took the decision to evacuate. Queen's closed on 28 September to pack up and prepare, and coaches, taxis and train seats were booked for the morning of 30 September. Eight hours before they were due to leave the Munich Agreement was signed for 'peace in our time'. It was decided, however, to go ahead with the evacuation and about fifty girls prepared for the journey north while the others remained in London:

> Friday, 30th September: The entrance hall at Queen's was full – full of people, full of cases, and overflowing with miscellaneous packages. Then everyone was bundled unceremoniously into taxis with their belongings. The hall was empty: the great exodus had begun. We arrived at Euston, where the yard was crowded with other refugees . . . there was a shocking shortage of porters, and we were forced to witness the pathetic spectacle of the preparatory department labouring under heavy burdens, and the boarders trying in vain to hold together unwieldy packages, tied up with rugs and string, in which their worldly goods were inadequately contained.

95

This and facing page: *Scenes during the evacuation of the School to Newlands in the Lake District, September to October 1938.*

Right: *Newlands House.* Below: *Entering the schoolroom – the village 'Institute'.*

The village of Newlands had just about everything they needed. There was an 'Institute' – a long wooden hut with a fireplace at one end and a smaller adjacent billiard room, in which they held classes, and a church at the other end of the village. Newlands guest house itself was a long two-storey converted mill house. They renamed the biggest room as the Common Room. 'This is a large room with a fire at one end, and a plentiful supply of orange basket chairs. There is a piano – for practising, singsongs – and last but definitely not least "Chopsticks"; shelves around the walls, and collapsible tables.' The girls took it in turns to study in the Common Room, the garden, and the Institute, but for much of the time the teachers took the girls out into the country – walking along lakesides, climbing mountains and descending on sleepy villages and towns for afternoon tea. Margaret Evans described one outing – dubbed as culture-hunting in Grasmere – a visit to Wordsworth's cottage:

> The cottage was charming. Its rooms were low and dark and although the kitchen would have been sternly frowned on by the sponsors of the servants' charter, most of us would have liked to live there – at any rate for a time. On its walls were hung very interesting portraits of the poet, his family, and friends . . . and we liked to visit the small hilly garden at the back with William's summer house, and the steps he and his brother made. In the museum which we visited there is a magnificent collection of Wordsworthian manuscripts and relics including Dorothy Wordsworth's journal written in a neat and beautiful hand which amazed us all.

After only a fortnight of their rural idyll Queen's girls were on the move again, back to Harley Street from where they watched the political and military events that led to the declaration of war on 3 September 1939.

Top left: *Map-reading on one of their many expeditions through the Lake District.*
Top right: *The Principal Gwendoline Holloway visits Newlands .*
Left: *Time off in Newlands.*

Queen's escaped serious damage during the war. However, on 30 September 1940, a bomb demolished the houses opposite the College and the blast hit the façade of numbers 43–47 with a force that knocked out all the windows, blew in doors, and brought plaster showering down in the front rooms. A block of modern flats now occupies the car park site.

CHAPTER SEVEN

QUEEN'S AT WAR

ON THE DECLARATION OF WAR SCHOOLS began to evacuate to places in the home counties, and, in the case of thousands of children, to Canada and the United States. Queen's girls were instructed to find their health certificates, pack their gas-masks and galoshes; and sixty-four girls, from the School and the College, were evacuated to Brackley, Northamptonshire, about 40 miles from London.

The Principal had rented Brackley House as a headquarters, and had negotiated with local schools to borrow some of their facilities including a gym, and a kitchen at Brackley High School for domestic science courses. Most classes, however, were held in a room above an ironmonger's shop. Games were played at Winchester House School. But such a well-intentioned whirligig of places and people must have taken its toll on the vigour and morale of the staff. The full-time teachers were of course billeted all over Brackley, while the part-timers had to battle their way to and from classes on a railway and bus system that was creaking with the pressure of the war effort.

Encouraged by the fact that London had not yet come under an air attack the College decided to hold some classes in Harley Street while keeping the main operation at Brackley. In the *Queen's College Magazine* a student described the beachhead made by a handful of students and staff in Harley Street:

'Digging for victory' at Brackley, Northamptonshire, 1940.

Miss Gwendoline Holloway, Principal from 1932 to 1940. She was responsible for organizing the College's evacuation to Brackley.

Miss Holloway's ration book.

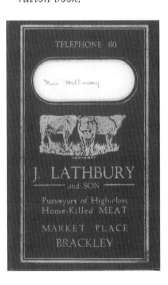

On 23 January 1940, a week after the new term had begun at Brackley, Queen's College opened its doors in Harley Street for what was probably the quietest first day of term since 1848. Most of the College buildings were closed up, number 47 being the only house used. One by one the students arrived to be greeted at the door by Miss Ceridwen Oliver, who constituted the entire full-time staff at Harley Street, since Miss Dean and Miss Kynaston spent three days a week each in London and Brackley. The place seemed very strange and empty; as we entered the large rooms we found ourselves talking in whispers that seemed to give back so vividly the many voices of those who had entered them in the past. We were in the unusual position of being new students with no established traditions to which we could adapt ourselves . . . some of the visiting staff were rather prejudiced in our favour so to speak, for having gone through long journeys in icy cold trains to get to Brackley, they arrived in sunny moods at Harley Street, pouring scorn and contempt on evacuation and all its attendant evils.

Miss Oliver, one of the nine staff who worked for Miss Kynaston throughout the war, had come to Queen's in 1932. For a remarkable thirty-one years she was secretary to the Principal and was still assisting with the archives and general enquiries through to the 1970s.

The *Magazine* article left out the factor that threatened to close the College completely. Some members of the Council felt that Harley Street would not be viable during the war, that central London would be the last place that parents would choose for their daughters, and that Brackley, with its mend-and-make-do approach, would not be able to compete with other well-established girls' boarding schools. A move was therefore made to close the College. The staff got wind of the plan, petitioned the Council, and, in the spirit of the first professors, many teachers offered to take a 50 per cent cut in their salary if the Council would agree to keep the College going. Some worked for no salary at all. Members of the Old Queen's Society generously contributed to an emergency fund, and it was decided to carry on if five or more pupils enrolled for classes. Only four pupils could be guaranteed, one from Brackley and three other new girls. Not quite enough. A small group of teachers hurriedly met and added another name to the list to meet the Council's minimum requirement. The 'phantom' student did not appear for classes for she was a private student of one of the teachers and was taught at home. The subterfuge was not discovered and the College carried on until it became legitimate when three more pupils enrolled.

Scenes during the College's evacuation to Brackley, Northamptonshire. Brackley House (centre). Left: *the gardeners ready for work; a lesson by torchlight* (top right); *at the entrance to Brackley House* (right).

College life in Harley Street was re-established in reduced circumstances. Number 45 along with the Pfeiffer Hall had been commandeered by the local branch of the ARP, whose wardens, with their gas-masks and fire-fighting equipment, came and went at all times of the day and night. The College could only use the house next door – number 47 – but even then the girls rattled around in floors of empty rooms and corridors. Elaine Kaye records that it was a curious little community: 'the youngest was 11, and alone constituted the School; she had private tuition. Three of them were about 16, but each one took a different course; secretarial, modern studies and 1 Junior; another student was 25 and took the senior course prior to taking up medicine. The last was a Czech refugee in her thirties who came to study English.'

The summer term saw a great improvement in the numbers. Forty girls signed up, among them Mary Churchill who during the early part of the term was given a day off to go to the House of Commons with her mother, 'to hear Daddy make his first pronouncement'. Although numbers were gradually building up Miss Holloway knew that the Council could not guarantee her salary in the foreseeable future, and accepted an offer to go to Alexandra College in Dublin as Principal. Joann Healey (1932–9) recalled that she resented Miss Holloway going off to Ireland. 'It seemed to us as young girls that she was deserting a sinking ship; however the intervening years have made me more sympathetic to her decision which must have been hard.' A contributor to the *Queen's College Magazine* swallowed her disappointment and tried to strike a positive note: 'It is a comfort to know that she is still in touch with Queen's, for Alexandra College was founded by Archbishop Trench, our second Principal.' Miss Holloway left Harley Street after fourteen years of dedicated teaching and leadership: 'Her gifts of intuition and sympathetic understanding enabled her to grasp the difficulties and problems of all with whom she came in contact, and she never failed to inspire even the shyest and most diffident.'

Miss A. M. Kynaston, a gifted English teacher who had been at Queen's for only two years, was appointed acting Principal until the Council made up its mind about the long-term future of the College. Miss Kynaston closed the temporary operation at Brackley and once again Harley Street became the focus of the College, but she had to wait until October 1942 before she was promoted to Principal.

The autumn term had just begun when London's worst fears were realized. The bombing of the capital began on 7 September 1940. The Woolwich Arsenal in South London was the first target. The German bombers followed it up with a ribbon of destruction along the Thames, hitting the riverside docks. British authorities estimated that over 1,400 incendiary bombs and 1,000 tons of high explosives rained down on the London docklands during the second week of September.

Miss Kynaston had a lucky escape. An account in Queen's College archives tells of one night before the beginning of the Michaelmas term when the block of flats in which she lived in North London was hit by a bomb. Her flat was wrecked but she got out with some of her possessions and took a taxi to Queen's. A member of staff who had arrived early, Miss Oliver, found Miss Kynaston and two of her friends having breakfast. They were in dressing gowns and were plastered with debris. As soon as the John Lewis department store was open they went to have their hair washed and to buy some clothes. That afternoon Miss Kynaston took

charge of the staff meeting as if nothing had happened.

On 30 September Queen's escaped total destruction by a matter of a few metres. A bomb demolished the houses opposite and the blast hit the façade of numbers 43–47 with a force that knocked out all the windows, blew in doors, and brought plaster showering down in the front rooms.

Queen's had to be evacuated for a second time. One of the members of the Council, Dr Stanley Marchant, was also Principal of the Royal Academy of Music and offered temporary accommodation in the Academy's buildings in Marylebone Road, only a few blocks away. Girls and staff put essential equipment into taxis, and, according to Rosalie Grylls, only about forty-five minutes of teaching time was lost. During their stay at the Royal Academy Queen's felt the blast of two more near-by bombs. All the windows at the back of the College were shattered and the bomb that fell in Portland Place in front of Broadcasting House blew out the boarded-up broken windows in the College buildings.

It took three weeks to make Queen's habitable again and when the girls and staff came back air raids had become part of College culture.

A tubular air-raid shelter, that looked like a long low Nissen hut, had

During air raids, classes continued at Harley Street in makeshift shelters in the main corridor of the College.

been built in the main corridor. About fourteen people could crouch inside and carry on classes during an air raid.

The girls and teachers also shared another shelter with the ARP men in the lower corridor. Ann Rea, a prefect in 1941, wrote about her experience in the shelter for the *Magazine* of that year:

> The mattress was down on the seats of the shelter and the one dismal globe was alight, so surreptitiously edging my way in I established myself under the light and spread my books around me. By crossing my knees, keeping my case balanced at a precarious angle and painfully craning my neck I could just see. Unfortunately somebody else had the idea of getting under the light on the other side of the bench, and sat down scattering my books wide. On my left, a long thin man was lying with a blanket tucked high under his chin. His nose moved gently up and down in time to his rhythmical breathing, twitching uneasily now and again . . . there was a strange silence as with glazed and unseeing eye everyone stared, and the silence was only shattered by song and laughter from the Auxiliary Fire Service men at the other end. A shout re-echoed 'Go little girls, all clear'. Books were collected and a scramble made for the door. Oh to be above ground! I looked down into our cold, unlit underground shelter. The long thin man still slept. The little fat man continued to drink tea, the singing continued loud and cheerful – in fact when the alert again went twenty minutes later, we returned to the same scene as before.

What is remarkable about the College during the early years of the war is the way the girls and the staff just carried on. They held meetings of the Debating Society and the Literary Society, Founder's Day was celebrated with a service at St Peter's Vere Street and a lunch afterwards at the College. Five students were learning fencing with Miss Macdonald, 'who is also doing very hush-hush war work' the girls whispered to each other. Old Girls came back to give the College moral support; classes contributed to the 'Spitfire Fund' and the Red Cross, and kept up their visits to the Lady Margaret Hall Settlement, a traditional charity for Queen's. By 1941 Diana Barnato Walker, a Queen's girl who was a débutante in 1936, had become one of the heroines of the Battle of Britain. She joined the Air Transport Auxiliary which was set up to transport people and mail around the country. More importantly the pilots were called upon to deliver new aircraft from factories to air-force bases. She climbed into the cockpits of fighter planes

The Senior Library with portrait of F. D. Maurice.

The main corridor (with a portrait of F. D. Maurice at the far end) a pleasant place to stop for a chat.

and twin-engined bombers, and before she had turned 22 years of age had flown 220 Spitfires and eighty other different types of plane without mishap.

In Harley Street those still at school even had the confidence to stage an elaborate mock trial in February 1941, when air battles were still being fought in the skies over the south-east of England:

> The senior arts room was arranged as a court, but the witnesses had no sooner finished making-up, than the air-raid warning sounded. We debated for some time as to whether or not we should hold the trial in the shelter, but fortunately the all-clear sounded after about ten minutes and we all hurried upstairs to the court where the counsels for the defence (Judy Montagu) and prosecution (Josephine Long), the jury, the clerk of the court (Priscilla Marks), and members of the public took their places, rising as the judge, resplendent in wig and gown, entered the room.

The editorial of the spring issue of the *Queen's College Magazine* in 1943 was full of optimism. The editor, Cynthia Morris, wrote glowingly of the way Old Girls had contributed to the war effort and of the spirit of independence and initiative shown by the girls who were still in Harley Street. 'During the past twelve months the number of students has almost doubled, and as always we have a lot of students from foreign lands, who, with their different traditions and customs, help to make for better understanding between nations, and also help to preserve the international and cosmopolitan atmosphere amid free thought, which has always been one of the chief attractions of this College.'

The Old Queen's Society, at its annual general meeting on 8 May 1943, also rejoiced in its very survival as an organization and noted that the Principal had given them the use of a room at 47 Harley Street from which to co-ordinate their activities. Old Queen's girls volunteered to do clerical work for the College, to take their turn at fire-watching, and despite the war began to consider how they would celebrate the College's centenary in 1948. 'In these days which have seen the destruction of so much of our heritage it is a privilege to belong to an institution which stands as a rock in a stormy sea. Those of us who have had the joy of visiting the College since its return home know that it still embodies that spirit which imparted by the Founder, has influenced many generations of students.'

Editions of the *Magazine* during 1943–4 are full of activities that suggest a perfectly normal routine: visits to the Regent's Park Open Air Theatre, a tennis tournament between the secretarial, science, and arts

students, lectures and talks in the Pfeiffer Hall, which the ARP had vacated in October 1943, piano recitals, and visits to various institutions including hospitals. Joyce Rackman, writing as theatre critic in the *Magazine* of 1944, comments in a vein that sounds remarkably familiar:

> The theatre at present is enjoying one of the greatest booms in its history, but, in my opinion, is not justifying the support it receives from the public. There seem to be few people, powerful in the theatre, who care for anything except their own pockets, with the result that they play for safety and present plays which entail few commercial risks. Because of this, most of the theatres are now showing imported or old musicals, dramatically unimportant farces, occasional plays by established writers – Noel Coward, Terence Rattigan, Emlyn Williams, for instance – and revivals of old plays. I think that if and when the National Theatre is founded, there should be a system similar to that of the Abbey Theatre in Dublin, where young playwrights attached to the theatre have a guarantee that their plays will be accepted and produced. Personally I do not believe that the English theatre is dead. It has been half asleep for years.

The V1 flying bombs in the summer of 1944 sent everyone back to the shelters. A few months later the even more terrifying V2s terrorized London. There was very little defence against them because these early rockets flew high and fast, and the only warning was silence in the sky when the engine cut out and the bomb was on its way down. College life carried on even if exams had to be conducted during air raids. Doreen Pierce remembered trying to do her School Certificate: 'On the morning of our first exam at 9.30 we heard the familiar wail of the siren. All through the examination we were given no peace, I do not think any of us were really frightened, we were too annoyed to be that, but somehow the staff and the building of Queen's helped to inspire confidence in us and we managed to survive unscathed.'

During the war the staff was rostered to do fire-watching. Mrs Fierz, who came back to Queen's as a teacher during the war, recalled that they all had lunch in the domestic science room, now the Bovell Sturge Laboratory, on the ground floor in number 45 Harley Street. 'During lunch someone used to sit in the Principal's office and if they heard a flying bomb they would ring a bell and the girls having lunch would all dive under the tables.' The College escaped a direct hit, but over 1 million houses in central London were destroyed or badly damaged. At the College the girls were safe. However, one pupil, Pauline Merz was killed when her house in Kensington took a direct hit. Only one member of the family survived: her mother who was an air-raid warden and was on duty during the raid. In memory of her daughter Mrs Merz gave the College £10,000 to build the laboratory that still bears her daughter's name.

Against formidable odds Queen's had survived the war, but took years to recover from its effects. Windows were still boarded up in Harley Street and there were rooms littered with rubble that took years to put back into order. A team of students and teachers began to clear up while preparations were made for the first Annual Gathering since 1939. Miss Kynaston apologized. 'May I say at this point how sorry we are that in view of the present world food situation we do not feel able to ask our audience to tea today. I do hope that the break with tradition, like the appearance of coloured dresses on the students which must be so distressing to Old Queen's eyes, may never occur again.' For many present that occasion must have seemed like nothing short of a miracle. She continued:

> The Council would wish to put on record the names of those members of staff who from the beginning to the end of this period never failed in their devotion and their courage: Miss Chaplin; Miss Shewell-Cooper; Mrs Bryson; Miss Dean; Miss Floyd; Monsieur Thiery; Miss Oliver (secretary) and Mrs Bailey (housekeeper).

Reporting to the 'Visitor', the Bishop of London, the Principal was able to say that every girl who entered for the London General School Examination in the College year (1944–5) passed. The lessons in air-raid shelters, the blitz and the blackout apparently steeled the girls who stayed. University places were gained by twelve students leaving at the end of the year, and two inspections by His Majesty's Inspector for secondary schools in London resulted in praise for most of what was happening at Queen's. Visiting lecturers during the year included Lady Megan Lloyd George and the composer Arthur Bliss.

The staff organized outings to picture galleries, museums and theatres, prompting the Principal to remark, 'It was strange to realize that hardly any girls in the School Certificate class had seen an Old Master and many had never been inside Westminster Abbey or St Paul's Cathedral.' Sonia Joseph put her feelings into verse:

Facing page and above: *Selection of the* Queen's College Magazine *covers, 1933–64.*

107

The misty sky is veiled with grey,
The shadows of departing day,
The sun forgets the world once more –
Forgets its sordidness – its war.
Remembers cornfields stacked with wheat
Forgets the marching tramp of feet,
Forgets until the next grey dawn
Until the white clouds deck the morn.
Then it remembers with regret
And almost feels it wants to set
But thinks we need it all the more –
Because of sordidness – and war.

Victory celebrations in London at the end of the war, 1945.

There can be no doubt that Mary Kynaston's determination and hard work lay behind the survival of Queen's. Her portrait in the corridor opposite the careers room on the ground floor of number 45 suggests a strong streak of steel behind bright-blue eyes. She was certainly a woman who pushed through problems to achieve her ends even if it meant bruising some egos on the way. When she took over in 1940 there was only a handful of girls. The College was on its uppers, but by 1943, when Stephanie Fierz came back with her science degree to teach, there were about 100 students, with more entering the College and School each term. The School for the younger girls, which had closed in 1940, reopened in 1942 and by the end of the war fifty-one girls up to the age of 14 were enrolled.

Mary Kynaston had reached the Principal's office by a hard path. She had come from a vicarage where money was short, and stayed on at her boarding school as a pupil teacher. In 1928 she enrolled at London's Birkbeck College and took a part-time course for a BA in English. She took a second degree in 1937, having spent several years researching the life of the eighteenth-century novelist Charlotte Lennox. She was, however, a very different character from her predecessor. Whereas Miss Holloway would often give lunches and entertain useful and engaging people, Miss Kynaston, although she did entertain, was more often at her desk. Her style of headship was, according to Joann Healey 'based on a clerical background of considerable self-restraint and personal discipline'. Dr Elaine Kaye, who taught at Queen's between 1954 and 1959, describes her as 'frugal' in the way she ran the College. 'Nothing was wasted, paper had to be used on both sides. A perfectionist, she made the staff draft their reports on the girls' work, which she would correct. The teachers would then have to do a final version for her approval.'

Former students remember her blue-lace dress that she wore at Annual Gathering and other College occasions. It was apparently beautiful, but she always wore it and the girls tended to giggle every time it came out. Stephanie Fierz remembers that some members of staff and pupils were frightened of her: 'she looks cold in her portrait, she was a bit of an iceberg'. Carole Bernard (1951–9) also remembers being terrified of her: 'She had a gimlet eye that never missed anything. She was a bit of an autocrat and wanted perfection.' Carole Bernard recalls that she was frightened of her all through her years at Queen's, but changed her mind on meeting her again as a young adult, 'she was a lovely lady, and very shy. That was her problem, and I had misjudged her character completely.' Everyone agrees that Mary Kynaston was a brilliant English teacher who drew the very best out of all her students. Joann Healey can still recite pieces of poetry that 'Kiny' taught her. 'She passionately believed in higher education for women and taught us poetry in such a creative way that I never forgot the verses. She wanted us to feel that the poetry we studied was part of our literary heritage that we could always call on.' In those post-war years Mary Kynaston laid down the foundations for the academic success of Queen's, along with other practical courses, that would underpin the College for decades to come. In the view of Elaine Kaye, 'Miss Kynaston built on the work that Miss Holloway had started without losing the individuality of Queen's that had been built up over generations.'

The centenary of the College was celebrated in 1948 with a calendar of events that included lectures, plays, an exhibition, and a visit from the patron, Her Majesty the Queen, who as the Queen Mother is still patron of Queen's College. The palace thoughtfully provided some advice on hats: 'It is not now necessary for women in academic dress to doff their caps in the presence of the Queen.' This relaxation of the rules turned out to be very practical, 'as some universities permit all women graduates to wear a soft cap fastened by a pin'.

The Queen arrived on 5 May wearing royal blue and a silver fox fur and was presented with a bouquet of flowers by one of the younger girls. There were speeches in the Pfeiffer Hall, including an address by Sir Frederick Maurice, F. D. Maurice's grandson, and a speech by the Queen herself. She expressed her views on the need for three Ds to supplement the three Rs: 'First, Discrimination – the ability to judge between the false

Miss A. M. Kynaston, Principal from 1942 to 1964.

and the true; second, Decision – the power to turn judgement into action; and third, Design – the art of giving practical form to a plan of action.'

Her Majesty saw the exhibition which included a model dressed as a schoolgirl of 1848. It had been lent by the Manchester City Art Gallery along with a magnificent doll's house furnished in mid-Victorian style. The Queen also visited the library where the girls from the domestic science department had gathered around a huge cake that they had made. Queen Elizabeth was invited to cut the first slice, a tricky operation seeing that the girls had shaped the cake to look like a book with its pages about the history of Queen's lying open.

The newspapers paid the centenary a lot of attention:

> Many of us became ardent collectors (probably for the first and last time in our lives) of press cuttings about ourselves. There were scores of articles, most of them uncritical in their praise of Queen's as a 'bluestocking incubator'. One journalist took the opportunity to write a profile of 'The Doctor's Street': 'Harley Street holds 150 large houses, most of them four storeys high. With only three or four exceptions, these houses are full of doctors – on an average, about ten doctors to a house.'

The *Tatler*, building on that theme took a tongue-in-cheek swipe at the street and its inhabitants:

> Meditating on the recent centenary of Queen's College for Women, Harley Street, we wondered what it must be like for that rosebud garden of girls to bloom – if one may put it delicately – in the very bosom of Britain's most expensive viscera-snatchers.
>
> An ex-alumna and a Harley Street boy alike have assured us that no harm befalls. The hirelings of Aesculapius, when a fair Queen's College undergraduate trips by their windows, tall as a lance and fresh as an April morning, like the girl in *Don Quixote*, certainly nudge each other, like the libertines in Pall Mall clubs, but for a different reason. 'Look, Gashworthy!' they cry licking their lips. 'There goes a perfectly sweet little re-entrant lesion of Boffin's Gland, or Hist Hackshaw! On the opposite pavement – a simply adorable compound recession of the outer coronary fibula.' In other words (explained this Harley Street chap) they look at girls not as girls but as potential slab fodder.

Miss Kynaston with prefects.

The centenary celebrations, like the 150th in 1998, reflected on some of the personalities who were either students or professors. There were lectures about F. D. Maurice, Charles Kingsley, Katherine Mansfield, Sophia Jex-Blake, Sir William Sterndale Bennett, and Dorothea Beale. The Drama Society put on a version of Alfred Tennyson's poem 'The Princess', and the girls took part in concerts. Annual Gathering in 1948 was held in the Wigmore Hall for the first time in the history of the College, so that all the visitors could be

HM the Queen and Miss Kynaston emerge from the College at the end of the Queen's visit to be greeted by a crowd of cheering girls.

Scenes around the school in its centenary year, 1948. Clockwise from above: Miss Jeffery's needlework class; a lesson in the gym. Prep time; the fencing class practising the Grand Salute; fencing had been taught at the College since the turn of the century.

accommodated. Gwendoline Holloway came back from Dublin, and addressed the gathering on the way Alexandra College, Dublin, had been inspired by Queen's College. Old Queen's students came back in droves to be present at such a historic occasion and to be there for the presentation of a portrait of Charles Kingsley, the College's first professor of English. The Old Queen's Association had commissioned a painter to copy the nineteenth-century one in the National Portrait Gallery. The copy hangs today in the Kynaston Library. The Senior student's address (Jean Leslie) stirred the emotions of the Old Queen's when she spoke lovingly of the inconvenient College buildings and how so many Old Girls present had talked about the warm and happy atmosphere that still prevailed in the College. 'If Frederick Maurice were to return today there are many things that would surprise him – the frenzied efforts of the prefects to keep the lunch queue in some sort of order,

and I speak with great feeling, and the equally frenzied efforts of the students to claim their lost property and their reluctance to pay appropriate fines.'

One of the initiatives by the Old Queen's Society that has become increasingly important to the College was the setting up of the Bursary Fund in 1951. The Old Queen's Society itself, founded in 1911, launched the fund to help with fees in hardship cases. The money was raised by bring-and-buy sales and through donations, and many families that have run into financial difficulties have been grateful to the fund. Resources had been very limited until 1963 when a substantial legacy was left by a London woman doctor, Ruby Olive Stern. A Trust Fund was then formed and with the continuing contributions from the annual Wine and Cheese Party, the growth of the Fund has become the most important thing that the OQS administers. It now stands at over £120,000 enabling five girls to be assisted with their fees each year.

Old Queen's have been very loyal to the College. Even in the 1950s the Principal had to get special forms printed for Old Queen's to register their month-old babies for the School. There are many families who go back several generations at Queen's.

During the late 1940s, and throughout the 1950s, Queen's offered a wide range of education. It was still possible to be a 'non-compounder' and just take one or two subjects. The Domestic Science department continued to offer its own popular courses and girls who wanted to learn secretarial skills had their own non-academic course to follow. Some girls finished off their academic career with the Modern Studies course, which was useful for girls who were not going on to university but were too young to be launched into London's social round or to find a more practical occupation. The School had abandoned the preparatory classes for the under-10s during the war and did not reintroduce them. The School course was therefore four years with about twenty pupils in each class. They moved up into the College's first Juniors for two years' work towards the GCE O-level examinations. At that stage they could choose to carry on academic study to A level joining either a Science or an Arts stream in the Senior College. Elaine Kaye, who taught in the College between 1954 and 1959 and went on to become an outstanding head of Oxford High School, recalled the mix of students at Queen's during the 1950s.

At this point a number of girls aged about 16 came from other schools to take these courses. Some of them came from small boarding schools

Scene in the College library, 1948.

Science lesson, 1948.

113

which could not provide anything beyond O level; some were not prepared to stay at boarding school any longer and wanted a day school. It was a mixture of students that . . . did call for great flexibility and hard work on behalf of the staff. Queen's was very different from other girls' schools in the 1950s. There were several male members of staff; a hangover from the nineteenth century when all the subjects were headed by a professor. Queen's also attracted girls from interesting backgrounds.

Miss Kynaston introduces Bishop Stopford to pupils at an Annual Gathering.

The mix which included Julia and Cressida Gaitskell, the Labour Party leader's daughters and the poet Louis MacNeice's daughter, Corinna, was further enriched by girls from all over the world who were daughters of diplomats. Susan Selwyn, *née* Leveson, went to Queen's in 1958: 'there were at least two Japanese girls, an American, an Indian, a girl from Pakistan, another from Afghanistan. It was my first real experience of people from other countries and they became my firm friends. But I have to confess that I spent the first day staring at the Japanese girls with their strange eyes.' Non-Christians did not have to attend theology classes and for Jews there were joint prayers in assembly one morning a week. Thereafter, Miss Margaret Blumenthal, a German teacher and a refugee from Nazism, took Jewish prayers in the Waiting Room. Susan Selwyn remembers witnessing a scene outside the Waiting Room during prayers when Miss Kynaston came along the corridor in her scholar's gown. 'Seeing two girls seated in the corridor she asked why they were not in prayers. One of the girls, about 16, replied that her parents were recently divorced. Her father, a famous show-business personality, was Jewish but her mother was not. The girl explained that she did not know which prayers she should attend. Miss Kynaston's voice was very kind and gentle and full of concern. After telling the girl how sorry she was she advised her to sit in the corridor daily and think about which group she would like to be with.'

With hindsight Carole Bernard is struck by the liberal nature of Queen's. 'It was after all a Church of England foundation and similar schools in London operated a quota system. No such restrictions at Queen's, and I am sure that the international atmosphere and religious tolerance had a lasting impact on our attitude to race and religion.'

One of the major innovations during the Kynaston reign was the acquisition of number 49 Harley Street, the turn-of-the-century red building at the northern end of the block. It was occupied by a doctor and his family who decided to give up the lease. The College's three Georgian buildings were by that time becoming uncomfortably full. As well as classrooms the houses still accommodated several members of staff, the Principal, and the boarding house. It was at this time that parents were asking for weekly boarding. The opening of number 49 in 1963 made expansion of the hostel possible, and also added another library, which today is called the Blue Library. The new house was appropriately named Kynaston House which is now the main entrance used by the girls.

When Miss Kynaston turned 60 in 1963, the chairman of the Council, Major Dent, called her in to discuss her future. Miss Kynaston expected to be invited to stay on for a few more years at least, but the Council came to the conclusion that after twenty-three years as Principal it was time for a change. Those who knew her at the time said that she took the decision badly and it took her some time to get over the shock. She retired at the end of the summer term in 1964 and kept in touch with her former students and her friends on the staff who often visited her at her home in Dorking. In February 1964, a former student and teacher, Mrs Stephanie Fierz was appointed Principal of Queen's College.

Portrait of Miss Kynaston which hangs in the College today opposite the Careers Room.

Modern girls in working mood in the Senior Library.

CHAPTER EIGHT
CHANGING TIMES

Stephanie Fierz, Principal of Queen's, 1964–83.

STEPHANIE FIERZ, AS WE HAVE SEEN IN PREVIOUS CHAPTERS, was herself a product of Queen's. She had been a boarder in 1927, then a science student who went to University College London. She had been drawn back to Queen's to teach during the war, but from 1949 to 1961 she and her husband Adrian lived in South Africa where she was a teacher. Returning to London after South Africa became a republic, she was in the right place at the right time to apply for the post of Principal of Queen's. Having read some glowing testimonials from South Africa, the Chairman of the Council, Major Dent, phoned Gwendoline Holloway who unhesitatingly recommended Stephanie and the deal was done. Major Dent was a collector of watercolours by English artists, particularly Rowlandson, and at the peak of the strawberry season each summer would invite the senior girls and their tutors to his house near Reading to see his collection. He remained as a wise sounding-board discreetly in the background for much of the new Principal's long term of office.

'When I took over, I found the College in good shape. The first thing I did was to loosen it up a bit; people needed to relax.' Mrs Fierz (she is still Mrs Fierz, even to those who have known her for over thirty years) encouraged the girls to look in if they wanted to discuss anything, and kept her door open throughout her nineteen years in Harley Street. 'The

117

children loved it and trusted me.' However, the frost of Miss Kynaston's disapproval was almost tangible when she came back to attend functions such as Annual Gathering. The former head confided to others, 'the girls had become too noisy, too easy-going'.

When Mrs Fierz took over there were still many no-go areas in the buildings. Many of the rooms at the top of the Harley Street houses still showed signs of damage from the war. Rooms were shut and littered with plaster from damaged ceilings. She had also inherited echoes of pre-war ways of doing things. By the 1960s the staff had their own waitress in the basement 'Bun Shop', the staff dining room. The Bun Shop, one of Queen's great institutions, was set up in the nineteenth century and lasted through until the war, when it functioned like a coffee shop for both senior girls and members of the staff who could buy doughnuts and sandwiches. The Bursar, Miss Alcock, lived on the premises and some felt ran the School as if she were the Vicereine of India. She had the Raj in her blood. Born in India of British parents, she divided and ruled at Queen's by dishing out little favours to tradesmen and members of staff. At meal times her edict ran that male members of staff were to get larger portions than female teachers.

James Hutchinson, one of the many new appointments made by Mrs Fierz in the 1960s, recalled that there was still a 'Professors' Room'. It is now the annexe to the Biology laboratory, and it was the last retreat of the dwindling band of male professors. More recent male teachers used to retreat here but now all the staff share the same staffroom. Jim Hutchinson came to Queen's partly because his tutor at King's, John Handford, was a 'Professor', the last one so named at Queen's. M. Jean Parzy taught French, and, during the war, had broadcast to occupied France on the BBC and worked as a member of General de Gaulle's staff in London. He always took his break, smoked his pipe and read *Le Figaro*, in the Professors' room. Perhaps the last user of this nineteenth-century sanctuary was David Bedford who was a music teacher. During his tenure he revolutionized music teaching and stunned the parents by getting the girls to compose modern music with the help of balloons that with wet squeaky fingers could be 'played' on cue. Queen's girls performed at the Royal Albert Hall and Queen Elizabeth Hall under his aegis. He was one of Stephanie Fierz's appointments and went on to become a composer of great distinction, following the tradition set by Sterndale Bennett.

When Jim Hutchinson was a postgraduate student, he needed some extra money and responded to a request from Mrs Fierz for a young

Major L. M. E. Dent, Chairman of the Council, 1967.

graduate teacher to help out. He got the job on the strength of his know-ledge of a particular Greek historian, not on his ability to teach. That requirement was never raised during his interview with the Principal or the Head of Classics. Aged 23 he faced his first class of teenagers; 'we drove away the last Classics teacher (she had disappeared in a flood of tears). How long are you going to stay?' As Senior Tutor today he looks back on that initiation with both amusement and horror. 'I must have been completely incomprehensible to them for about 18 months as I taught myself to teach!'

Deputy Principal, James Hutchinson, who joined Queen's in the 1960s.

But Queen's began like that a century and a half ago with academics from King's College treating 12-year-old girls like undergraduates. That tradition has gone, no one gets a teaching job today without adequate training, but the tradition of recruiting from King's College is still alive. Counting them up Mr Hutchinson reckoned 'there are four or five teach-ers on the staff at the moment who were at King's, as well as Margaret Brunyate, the College Secretary, who used to teach at Goldsmith's, who helped so much to improve our efficiency'. The link is strengthened by the continued inclusion of a current member of King's College's staff on the Council.

The staff at Queen's in the 1960s and 1970s had a certain stamp. They were not career teachers but people who found themselves drawn to Queen's. Mrs Fierz's first appointment was Julia Roskill, later Librarian and a member of the Council. She followed Susan Reynolds who left to teach history at Lady Margaret Hall, Oxford; Julia then introduced Celia Goodhart, another of Mrs Fierz's appointments. She came as a part-time History teacher in 1966 and was bowled over by the place. She had spent her schooldays in a grim missionary boarding school. Her father was the second Baron Hemingford, himself a missionary who then chaired the Africa Bureau and later became a Lord Lieutenant. It was her mother who really encouraged her to go to university. Celia Goodhart graduated from St Hilda's College, Oxford (founded by Dorothea Beale), and after a career in the Civil Service, which included a stint at the Treasury and a high-powered job at the Ministry of Agriculture, married and gave up her civil service career at a promising moment. Teaching A level fitted better with the demands of rearing babies, and she was greatly impressed with the School. 'There was no uniform, the girls were treated in an adult civ-ilized way, there was warmth and friendliness which was very unusual in a girls' school in the 1960s. It was an interesting, international place that seemed to turn out remarkable, independent young women.' At that time

Outdoor lesson.

119

the international mix at Queen's was strengthened by a contingent of Greeks, the daughters of shipping tycoons, including Aristotle Onassis's daughter, Christina. Queen's was their London school until the exiled King Constantine chose to settle in the United Kingdom and set up a Greek school in England.

Queen's also had a resident community of intellectuals; teachers who lived in flats scattered throughout the Harley Street houses. Patricia Davies, a graduate of St Hilda's College, Oxford, who became Head of Classics, had the most memorable apartment. Hers was like the rooms of an Oxbridge don; the walls lined with books and with erudite papers scattered about. She would have made a perfect don. Colleagues would be invited for tea and groups of senior girls sometimes went up for classes. By 1980 there was no more room for flats except for the succession of caretakers and hostel wardens. One of Pat Davies's colleagues, Jane de Swiet, went on to become Head of the Classics department of City of London School and then Headmistress of Henrietta Barnett School, which tops the maintained-sector league tables as often as not. Enid Greenslade, the music teacher, lived on site from 1946 as did the Bursar and Julia Roskill. Miss Lambert, who was Head of Biology and Senior Tutor from 1968 until she retired in 1982, had a great eye for detail and made sure that the organization of the College ran smoothly. She told the story that her father had been given new penicillin as an experiment by Alexander Fleming, possibly sparking her lifelong interest in biology. Margaret Blumenthal was a tremendous favourite with teachers and girls as was Beatrice Burstall: 'both were much loved and very civilizing influences' says Celia Goodhart. 'The children also loved being given French orals by Mrs Fitz Gerald whose daughter-in-law Jenny has presided over the libraries with the same concern for the girls since about 1987.' Many of the teachers gave 'lectures' at which the girls were supposed to take notes. They were not spoon-fed by being given photocopied notes. Cindy Polemis, one of the Greek contingent, who was a Senior College student (1973–5) recalls that she felt at home when she went up to Oxford to read History. 'I know that many of my friends from other schools had a problem in dealing with the style of University dons. I was fine. I was used to the type and their ways of teaching because of the teachers at Queen's'.

Mrs Fierz also appointed the Olympic rower Tessa Millar as Head of Physical Education, a post she holds to this day with great distinction. The Principal was also introduced by Celia Goodhart to three people who have given much to Queen's over a long period of time: one was Lindy

Language laboratory.

Foord, the daughter of novelist Rayner Heppenstall, a distinguished linguist who became Senior Tutor following Yvonne Brett's retirement in the summer of 1998. Helen Maclennan and Sally Stopford brought a transatlantic touch to the teaching of History and English, being graduates of Radcliffe – one of America's Ivy League universities – before attending Oxford and Cambridge respectively. Sally Stopford is the daughter-in-law of the Bishop of London who was the College Visitor in the 1960s.

In this interesting staff room another American, poet Terry Bagg, used to spar with Judith McDonald, a charismatic philosophy graduate from Trinity College, Dublin, whose interpretations of Milton enlivened many a Bun Shop lunch. Judith was passionate about her subject and although volatile in her relationships, she is remembered by staff and pupils as one of the kindest people you would ever hope to meet. In similar charismatic mould was Shankara Angadi, who had read History at Cambridge and turned up at Queen's to teach between theatrical ventures. A self-confessed eccentric, he had taken over from his father, arranging visits to Europe by music, dance and theatre companies from Asia. In 1972 he needed to teach as a stopgap, was hired by Mrs Fierz and stayed. Sadly his time at Queen's came to an end when he was accused of having sexual relations with a girl at the School. He was subsequently acquitted but decided to leave the School. The Director of Studies and Head of History until 1999, he recalled that one of the impressive aspects of Queen's was the way the girls were treated. 'They were not encouraged by Mrs Fierz to believe that they were children who had to obey adults, which meant that the girls had to learn to take responsibility for their actions at a very early age.' Sometimes, however, the staff would become exasperated with the Fierz regime of almost total tolerance, especially when, in cases of last resort, a naughty girl might be sent by the form teacher to explain herself to the Principal. But Mrs Fierz found it extremely difficult to dish out punishment, especially if the miscreant could make her laugh. She would talk the problem over and then get the girl to wait long enough to make it look as if she were getting the sharp end of the Principal's tongue. Such an admonition often ended with the girl returning to her class trying to hide more than a bit of a smirk.

There were some rules: girls must never tell a lie, or smoke, or wear anything like trousers. Trouser suits, Mrs Fierz believed, were excessively common, and if the girls started wearing them the younger members of the staff might follow suit. That could not be tolerated. If they wanted to wear trousers there were special days when the girls could donate money

Music studio.

The Queen Mother, patron of the College, on her visit in 1972 to open a new science laboratory.

Queen's drama students took The Beggar's Opera *to the Edinburgh Fringe, 1995.*

to charity for the privilege. Almost anything else fell within the dress code. One pupil from that period used to come to school in a big rugby shirt and furry boots, and that was all; the shirt counted as a dress of a sort and was therefore within the dress code.

There were many occasions when Mrs Fierz would react instantly to a pupil's predicament. Michele Wade, later to become an actress and now presiding over a famous Soho patisserie, was at Queen's in the early 1970s and in the middle of a family upheaval she announced that she would have to leave. Her parents were selling their house in Harley Street where Michele lived. 'Don't worry old thing, you can come and live with us.' Mrs Fierz meant it and soon Michele was in the Fierz's sitting room on a spare bed until the family sorted out their housing problem. The unusual informality at Queen's did not mean that it was like a St Trinian's out of control. In the 1960s and for much of the 1970s Queen's went from strength to strength. Such was the demand for places that there was a lengthening waiting list. Non-academic subjects, secretarial and domestic science, had to be dropped in favour of strengthening the Senior College. Celia Goodhart believes that 'during the 1960s and early 1970s Queen's was a high-powered place that had a pioneering role in Sixth Form education offered by girls' schools'. Mrs Fierz continued the trend established by Miss Kynaston which enabled girls who had perhaps been to limited girls' schools to enter Queen's, take their A levels and go on to university. A significant proportion of leavers went to university and Queen's successfully encouraged girls to aim for Oxford and Cambridge. Cindy Polemis remembers that in her year, 1975, at least half a dozen girls got into Oxbridge.

Queen's was one of the first girls' schools in London to set up a computer network to be used in teaching. By 1983 Queen's had probably the first computer network – whose file server was a tape recorder! Working with IBM, Jim Hutchinson also pioneered the use of links to a mainframe computer to cut down on the time-consuming job of checking the timetable. In Mrs Fierz's time two new Science laboratories were built and with the help of the Sainsbury family, whose daughter Sarah was a pupil, the stage area of the Pfeiffer Hall was redesigned. This was opened by the College Patron Her Majesty Queen Elizabeth the Queen Mother in 1980. She had visited the College before, for the Centenary celebrations in 1948 and again in 1972, on the occasion of the centenary of Maurice's death when she opened the new Merz laboratory.

Music and drama had long been features at Queen's. In the late 1960s,

Night Child, *a production at Queen's, transferred to the Old Vic, 1978.*

Hermione Lee, now Professor of English at Oxford, performed in an outstanding chorus in *Antigone*. A magnificent *Midsummer Night's Dream* was produced by Jane Daly with music composed specially by David Bedford. Performances of *The Importance of Being Earnest* and *St Joan* are remembered to this day. Inheriting this mantle Shankara Angadi then mounted a number of ingenious productions with original music and increasingly complex staging, sound and scenic effects. Parents weighed in to help and generations of pupils have become proficient in stage lighting and sound technology. One of his productions was such a success that parents raised £15,000 to transfer it to the Old Vic.

More recently there have been outstanding productions of *The Tempest* and *Dido and Aeneas*, conducted by William Leigh Knight and directed by George Freeburn who left Queen's to join the Royal Opera. An all-female *Macbeth* produced by Roland Taylor achieved acting of astonishing maturity, and when they did *The Beggar's Opera* it went on to the Edinburgh Festival. So too did *Insurrection*, written for Queen's by James Rose who also produced it in collaboration with Roland Taylor, continuing the line of talented composers heading the Music department. This piece particularly captured the Queen's spirit since it was about the suffragettes and female emancipation.

The Music department's magnificent jazz concerts, 'regarded dubiously by our neighbours because of the decibels they generate', says the Bursar, demonstrate the exceptional versatility and stage presence of Queen's girls who are always ready to perform. Meanwhile Christine Lax's concerts on more classical lines testify to the long choral tradition and growing strength of individual instrumental performance. She has pioneered informal concerts after school in which girls perform in public for the first time alongside established musicians.

In 1997 the sesquicentennial celebrations opened with an Angadi/Rose version of Gilbert and Sullivan's *Princess Ida*, originally written partly to mock Queen's and certainly the education of women. Not surprisingly a number of Queen's girls over the years have been inspired towards the theatre and film including Emma Freud, Sophie Ward, Susannah Wise, Caroline Johnson, Jennifer Ehle, Katharine Schlesinger, and Kathryn Hunter (known at Queen's as Kathryn Hadjipateras). Others have gone on to pursue careers in the pop world. Miki Berenyi and Emma Anderson formed the band 'Lush' and Amanda Rootes plays with 'Fluffy'.

Towards the end of the 1970s Queen's reputation for its eccentricities became stronger than its academic record. Celia Goodhart argues that the School had changed, and that 'the main problem was that the girls were not made to work hard enough; perhaps it had become a bit too liberal in the late 1970s'. The architect of almost two decades of remarkable liberal education, Stephanie Fierz, looking back on her stewardship agrees that, by the time she was ready to retire, Queen's needed to change gear. The new Principal, Patricia Fleming, who arrived in 1983, could not have been more different.

Mrs Fierz was a hard act to follow; for nineteen years she had treated the staff and the pupils like her own extended family. Mrs Margaret Kearney, one of the domestic employees, who has just retired after

Mrs Patricia Fleming, Principal of Queen's from 1983 to 1990.

twenty-five years at the School, remembers her with great affection to this day. Moreover the senior girls got up a petition imploring her not to retire. But to no avail. Mrs Fierz claims that once she had made up her mind it was time to go she did not waver. But she had a hand in the choice of successor. Mrs Fierz did not agree with the Council's first choice and Patricia Fleming, the runner-up, was offered the job.

She was an experienced teacher, well qualified to lead Queen's into another era. Ulster born and educated at Trinity College, Dublin, she spent most of her career teaching in London, first in state secondary schools and later at St Paul's Girls' School. Before applying to become Principal of Queen's, Mrs Fleming had worked on developing syllabuses at the London Regional Examining Board. Queen's impressed her: 'I liked the individuality of the school, the way Mrs Fierz's door was always open and the fact that she knew the name of every single child in the school.' But it was very different from any other school in which the new Principal had taught. 'There was no co-ordinated academic policy and no organization to deal with the pastoral side of the school's life.' Looking back, Jim Hutchinson agrees that Queen's needed to change. 'The College was inward-looking – we did not go to other schools or to conferences and we had no idea how other educational institutions were run.'

The main stairway –
a central feature of the
College since its foundation.

The new Principal also decided to spend money on the building. Money had not been spent but husbanded by very careful housekeeping over the past two decades by Mrs Fierz who for example kept the central heating low or off. But Mrs Fleming declared that the reserves were to be spent on the buildings. A new Bursar was appointed and major construction works were undertaken. Classrooms were enlarged so that the junior end of the School could have larger classes. The organ was installed in the Hall – to the delight of Murray Stewart, then Head of Music and now a well-known conductor. At this time the Sixth Form began to shrink, partly because of competition from other schools. Boys' public schools had begun to cream off the brightest girls from both the state and private sectors and Queen's took the decision to enlarge the intake at the bottom of the school to keep the numbers up.

A major piece of reconstruction caused the destruction of the nineteenth-century science laboratory, the first built for a girls' school. It had a high ceiling with a skylight and was a rare example of a period chemistry laboratory complete with polished wood benches, brass taps and porcelain basins. It would have been a perfect museum piece. Above it the New Floyd Room was created, with doors that open out on to the main

Geography lesson.

Modern girl in artistic mood.

floor of the Pfeiffer Hall; today it is a computer laboratory. The Art department was re-equipped with a print room, and a photographic dark room added, and a new Modern Languages room was built over the old Geography room. Like her predecessors, Mrs Fleming introduced new teachers to the College and made some very good appointments. Two first-class arrivals in the studio to teach Art are still at Queen's – Rose Martinez, art historian, artist, singer and actress and the Welsh painter and photographer Cheryl Drower. Rose Martinez today holds together the Junior College by her pastoral care, while Cheryl's skills with the camera provide the College with a fine photographic archive, each year producing a rogues' gallery of pupil snapshots to help staff identify them. Each year the exhibitions enable staff to admire the talents of pupils and some of their best work adorns the corridors. Entry to top Art Colleges seems to be an almost automatic progression.

As Head of Classics there arrived from the maintained sector Valerie Potter (now a member of Council) whose career and personality peculiarly suited her to become the first Senior Mistress, patiently nurturing pupils through pastoral crises into calmer waters. Anne Smith later joined the newly created pastoral team as School Mistress; with characteristic modesty, she never spoke of her considerable athletic achievements. She was the pioneer of women's middle-distance running in this country, and she set the world record of 4 minutes 37 seconds for the mile in 1967. Her tragically sudden death in 1993 shook the College to the core but the grief of pupils taught the College how much the staff are valued, as the obituaries in the national press and the Principal's tribute at her memorial service made clear.

Another tragic death, that of Vivienne Tyrrell at an even younger age, had led to the arrival of Cambridge-educated Fiona McIntosh to take over the Geography department. She became the British No. 1 fencer and a member of the national Olympic team. Queen's girls tend to dominate the schools' fencing championships; 'once they'd defeated all the girls' schools they started on the boys' says Celia Goodhart who, when Fiona McIntosh's husband was posted to South Africa and she left in 1996, appointed her successor who was also top British fencer, Lucy Harris. Tessa Millar completes the list of athletes and sportswomen – she rowed for Britain in the Los Angeles Olympics and continues to coach Great Britain men's lightweight team. Until Anne Smith's death Queen's had three Olympic women athletes serving on its staff – a prowess all the more remarkable for a school which never had its own playing fields.

There is a strong tradition of fencing at Queen's College, and the girls tend to dominate the schools' fencing championships today.

At first the staff all supported her plans for change but in a short time many of the members of staff that Mrs Fleming had inherited became disaffected. They particularly disliked the proposal to disband the Committee of Education which dated back to the foundation of the College, a policy-forming group of senior teachers who advised the Principal on academic matters. Mrs Fleming wanted to increase its numbers from five members to ten so that all departments could be represented. The enlargement was not a problem, but dropping of the name was: it was seen as an unnecessary break with the past. 'It took a very long time to introduce, perhaps the most difficult change I attempted during my time at Queen's.' Indeed she had threatened to resign if the Committee was not wound up and reconstituted.

Mrs Fleming's changes to the management structure, the introduction of new staff and the redeployment of existing teachers created much discontent in the staff room. Yvonne Brett, a former civil servant who had taught in Africa, and appointed by Mrs Fierz to run the Modern Languages department, became a central figure at this difficult time in her role as Dean. She was shrewd and wise when it came to solving problems with the curriculum and acted as a peace-maker throughout a very turbulent period in the staff room. According to Jim Hutchinson, 'they were dark days, very depressing. I had never known anything like the

Netball at Regent's Park.

atmosphere in the staff room, the changes led to a lot of ill-feeling.'

Was the main problem a personality clash between senior members of the staff and the new Principal? Patricia Fleming in retrospect thinks not. 'It was not a personality clash, it was an ideological clash over the way the school should be run that upset many of the staff.' The Principal's working relationship with the Council was not harmonious either; her plan to launch an appeal for funds to build science laboratories on the roof was vetoed as the Council felt that the time was not right and the plans too costly.

As in most independent-sector schools the Council of Queen's College has never been actively engaged in the day-to-day business of the School. The most recent chairman of the Council, Mrs Marie Patterson CBE, a former chairman of the Trades Union Congress, remembers Queen's College Council meetings in the mid-1980s as 'rather dreary, long-winded, with the chairman spending hours and hours on detail'. The Council's role then, as it is today, was to take care of the finances, set the fees and to appoint the Principal. The Royal Charter of 1853, under which they work, gives the Principal total control of the running of the School. However, in 1987 the Council became embroiled in a controversy over Mrs Fleming's decision to sack a long-serving teacher who was over the age of retirement.

The teacher appealed to the Council on the grounds of unfair dismissal and was reinstated. It was a blow to Mrs Fleming who accepted the rebuff and carried on until the question of her retirement at the age of 60 was raised by the Council in 1990. She was not asked to extend her term of office, resigned and reached an agreement with the Council to go in December 1990, before the end of the academic year. The resignation of a Principal who was popular with many girls and their parents resulted in the Queen's College Parents' Association (set up by Mrs Fleming as soon as she arrived) asking questions about the running of the School. Some parents were also concerned about the patchy results for girls taking science subjects and blamed them on a lack of the latest equipment in the laboratories. Attempts by the Parents' Committee to get satisfactory answers from the Council failed. When the Council announced that Lady Goodhart had been appointed Principal, the Parents' Committee, having discovered that her only teaching experience had been part time at Queen's in the 1960s and 1970s, wondered if she was the right woman for the job. Some parents on the Committee strongly objected and would have liked to see Mrs Fleming reinstated.

Returning from hockey in Regent's Park.

Jim Hutchinson with girls on the stairs in Summer 2000.

Left: *biennial trip to Greece: Tiryns.*

Below: *visit to the Dome, spring 2000.*

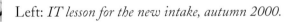

Left: *IT lesson for the new intake, autumn 2000.*

Below: *informal concert.*

The Queen's College Parents' Association Committee invited the newly appointed chairman of the Council, Sir Peter Leslie, to address a parents' meeting. As he was unable to be present, a member of the Council deputized for him, and, addressing a large audience, told them in no uncertain terms that the running of the School was a matter for the Council and not for the parents. The Parents' Committee angrily called an Extraordinary General Meeting and proposed a motion of no confidence in the Governing Council and the newly installed Principal. The motion was lost owing to a persuasive speech by Sir Peter Leslie who was able to reassure parents about Celia Goodhart's plans for upgrading the science laboratories, with the help of Fiona Frais, then Head of Science, and the College Architect, Anthony Kyrke-Smith. Eloquent appeals by several members of the staff including the Principal, Jim Hutchinson and Shankara Angadi turned round most of the parents, some of whom were supportive anyway.

It was an uncomfortable time for both the staff and the Council, for which Sir Peter accepts some of the blame. 'The parents were uneasy about Mrs Fleming leaving before the end of the academic year. They thought that we were being unfair to her and I, as a newly appointed chairman of the Council, along with other members, was slow to see and to react to the depth of feeling among the parents.' But Celia Goodhart says, 'Queen's College owes a very great deal to Sir Peter Leslie. He was an ideal chairman, especially at that time, and he gave me perceptive and strong support and much of his time in my early years, understanding exactly the pressures put upon headmistresses at the best of times, and reacting to this manipulation of parents with piercing insight and shrewd calmness.' He was also the prime mover behind significant changes that were made to the Council in the early 1990s. Many of the older members resigned and new younger men and women with a wider range of experience were appointed. The Council also decided to include in its ranks two parents who currently had children at the School. The Council, then consisting of seventeen members and listed on page 146, 'has a good mix of expertise and personalities', in the opinion of Marie Patterson. She has a no-nonsense approach to getting things done, believes that the Council works well and that 'if anything were to go wrong at the school, I, as chairman of the Council, would not hesitate to call a special meeting and take any necessary action'.

Celia Goodhart arrived in January 1991 to find not only all the parental unease, but deep divisions among the staff. A more inauspicious

Nurse's room.

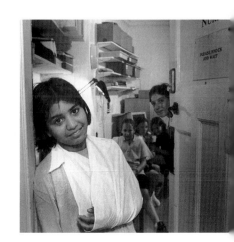

A visit to Nurse Hutchison's surgery appears to be a not unpleasant experience.

Lady Goodhart, who is Chairman of the Oxford Society, and was Principal of Queen's College from 1991 to 1999.

start for a new Principal could hardly be imagined. She had of course known Queen's well in the 1960s and 1970s when she had taught A-level History for ten years, but nothing then could be compared with the sour and volatile atmosphere she inherited. In the time since she taught at Queen's she and her husband Sir William Goodhart QC, now Lord Goodhart, had thrown themselves into politics. They both contested parliamentary seats for the SDP and Liberal Alliance, Celia for Kettering on two occasions in 1983 and 1987. She also stood as a candidate for the European election of 1984, again for the SDP.

A series of party political jobs followed: Chairman of the SDP's Environment Policy Group; Chair of Women for Social Democracy; member of the SDP and Liberal Democrat National and Policy Committees. She had also served as a governor of several schools including Godolphin and Latymer School in West London and on government-appointed and hospital ethical committees. Other interests outside politics included serving as Chairman of the North Thames Gas Consumer Council, Chairman of Youth Clubs UK and President of the School Mistresses and Governesses' Benevolent Institution (formerly the Governesses' Benevolent Institution) which gave birth to Queen's College in 1848. She still holds this position which provides a most happy coincidence once again linking the SGBI with Queen's.

The experience of the rough and tumble of politics turned out to be useful in her new career running Queen's. *Queen's News* was started by her in 1991 to keep the parents informed about what was going on. 'If parents are going to gossip about Queen's, let's give them something positive to talk about,' said Jim Hutchinson, the editor, whom the Principal describes as 'a frustrated journalist'. After a few frosty months the Parents' Committee realized that they were dealing with a new tough Principal, whose strengths as an administrator were sorely needed in an educational world that was becoming increasingly complex. One aspect of the new Principal's taut and sometimes gritty management style came as a shock to the older girls. The open-door policy of the two former Principals was abandoned for an appointment system. She saw College pupils on a one-to-one basis for an individual interview each year. Did the girls at first think that she came across as pretty formidable? 'I think perhaps they did, maybe it's because I'm six foot and large. But I don't court popularity. As for the end of the open-door, the Principal's job is a more complex and busy one than it used to be and you cannot spend time chatting with people – there just isn't time.' The girls, however, found that when they did capture Lady Goodhart's time, they got her undivided attention for as long as it took to deal with a problem, and very often an immediate response. While a girl was with her Lady Goodhart was quite likely to make phone calls on her behalf, call for files and even summon teachers. The girls were often surprised that there was an unsuspected warmth and sympathy. Parents got the same treatment when they went to discuss problems, although some left in high dudgeon, after a stream of 'straight talking' that was characteristic of the Principal's approach to what she described as 'feckless parents'.

Lady Goodhart's understanding and sympathy for adolescent girls (one of her own daughters, Laura, was at Queen's in the 1980s) came through clearly during the often emotionally charged cases dealt with by the pastoral committee. Made up of the school nurse and three senior members of staff, Lindy Foord, Rose Martinez and Antonia Lang, and chaired by the Principal, they spent the best part of every Wednesday afternoon talking about, and trying to solve, problems that girls were facing at School and at home. Such crises ranged from bullying, eating disorders, serious illness, death in the family or the shock waves generated by parents in the middle of a divorce.

One of the first recommendations of the new Principal was a swingeing increase in fees: 20 per cent for the first year followed by 15 per cent the following year. As well as stabilizing the College's finances it enabled Lady Goodhart to go through the place with a pot of paint. 'I mind passionately about what things look like. When I came here it was all a bit grey, now it is much jollier, with colour everywhere. We also had to spend a large amount of our reserves on the roofs which leaked like a sieve in places.' There was a landing on one of the staircases that had a shallow lens in the middle of the stone, worn by the constant action of dripping water in the winter. The science laboratories were greatly improved and decorated with pastel colours, including the three that are named after pioneering women scientists from Queen's: Sophia Jex-Blake, Ethel Truman, and Emily Bovell Sturge. The self-contained music area that was created at this time is named after Enid Greenslade.

Colourful floral wallpaper started appearing, even in parts of the building into which parents and governors never venture. But the main corridor in the College, with richly coloured wallpaper enhanced by indirect lighting was Lady Goodhart's *pièce de résistance*. At the time various members of staff predicted that some girls might be tempted to enrich the floral designs with ideas of their own, but not one graffito appeared. In a

Nowadays the Principal's office opens on to this area.

131

About to descend Gaping Gill pothole on the Junior Yorkshire trip.

School trip to the Orkney Islands.

flurry of improvement the dining room in the basement was reorganized and enlarged with a cafeteria system. New junior common rooms were created out of the basement lockers and more space added by enclosing a small outside area. In 1993 that area had to be underpinned at great expense as it was found to have been built without any foundations – on sand.

The decision to close the boarding house was also a landmark in the history of Queen's. The new Bursar, Eva Chesswas, took up her post in 1993 and found that the boarding house was not breaking even. The demand for such accommodation in central London had been slowly evaporating. 'We were down to six boarders at one stage, and the decision to close the hostel, which occupied most of Kynaston House, gave us at least a dozen more rooms to use for meetings, classes, offices, studies for teachers, a room for the school nurse and a girls' senior common room.' The loss of the boarding house was perhaps inevitable, but some day girls regretted its demise; they felt that Kynaston House had lost its heart and that without the boarders the lively atmosphere of the school dwindled away too early in the afternoon as classes ended and everyone went home.

One of Queen's academic strengths is language teaching. Whereas many comparable schools have pared down their range of both classical and modern languages (which is why *ab initio* courses are commonly on offer at universities) Queen's still offers A levels in Greek, French, German, Italian and Russian. It does so in the two language laboratories installed in the mid-1990s, one of which is equipped with satellite television. In response to a school inspector's recommendations that more staff should go on refresher courses, Lindy Foord took a sabbatical year and went to Tokyo to study Japanese; on her return the school was able to offer beginners' Japanese for the first time. 'Hiragana' and 'Katakana' charts are to be seen on the Language Laboratory walls, and a Japanese sketch, complete with kimonos and chopsticks was a feature in the last Polyglot evening. The Polyglot itself, a biennial event and a Queen's invention, offers a cabaret of poetry, song and drama in every language taught at the school, followed by an international buffet provided by the Queen's College Parents' Association, who also assist pupils who might otherwise not be able to go on the school trips that have become an important feature of school life over the last twenty years.

As many as eighty visits might take place in a single year, and each year several foreign visits have been arranged to places such as Morocco, Israel, the Cevennes, Spain, Italy, Greece and nearer home the Orkney

Islands. Financial assistance for these trips is sometimes made available from the Fleming Fund or the Queen's College Parents' Association. The Pilkington Trust was started by the Pilkington family, one of whose members, Cynthia Rumboll, was President of the Old Queen's Society for twenty-five years. The Trust provides generous funds for girls to travel during their gap year, and will match the money raised by the girls pound for pound. The staff travel as well. Lady Goodhart encouraged her staff to go on training courses and to attend educational conferences. Teachers started to visit other schools and universities, and the Principal herself was in demand as a speaker at national and international conferences.

Queen's competes with other schools in Mathematics Olympiads and Latin and Greek Reading Competitions, which they win year after year. The girls take part in debates, including the Observer Mace, and Dr Eleanor Relle, an outstanding teacher who grew up in Australia and who finished her education at Newnham College, Cambridge, where she taught for a time, is largely responsible for the latter triumphs. The classics successes owe much to Sarah Harrison, Head of Classics.

During the 1990s Queen's moved into a higher gear. More choice of subjects was available, the average age of the staff fell and academic standards rose. Lady Goodhart developed a large Senior Management Team, 'so that the College was run in a less Principalian way: I consulted more and I delegated so more people knew and understood what was going on'. A weekly staff briefing meeting helped to make the College more efficient. 'We even cracked the caretaker and maintenance problem.' Matt Kevin is much in evidence around Queen's and 'much valued'. In 1994 the College volunteered to have an inspection, its first since the early 1980s. The Deputy Principal, Jim Hutchinson, had moved heaven and earth to bring up to date all the procedures and to provide the mountain of paperwork required. The place had never looked so sharp and tidy and everyone was performing to maximum effect – the girls' behaviour was exemplary when the inspectors looked in on some classes. On the first morning of the inspection, which everyone thought was going very well, the police unexpectedly arrived to interview a couple of tearaways who had been caught shoplifting at John Lewis's. It couldn't have happened at a worse time, the day was surely doomed, but instead of writing the place off as a den of thieves the inspector complimented the College on the prompt way crises were dealt with. The report was very good: the inspector was full of admiration for the girls and commented that the staff was second to none. One of the main recommendations, that a full-time nurse

Assembly.

Waiting for the bell in the main corridor.

The new Junior Common Rooms – in the basement – are also used for lunching in.

should be added to the staff, was quickly implemented.

There were major changes to the curriculum during the 1990s. Science teaching was reorganized so that the dual award course is followed. Further Maths, Computing and Theatre Studies were added at A level. Smaller classes introduced at the same time – from twenty-eight to twenty – made a big difference to teaching and results. At the same time the number of classes was increased to three so that now the intake at 11 years of age could be increased to sixty.

The 1990s brought a change in the attitudes of parents towards education and the schools they selected for their children. 'I'm paying the fees and I want results' summed up the attitude, according to Jim Hutchinson. 'In the late 1980s and early 1990s there was much competition for the Sixth Form and clever girls who left to go to other schools before taking their A levels could and did affect the School's position in the league tables. Parents took notice and it had an impact.' The first league tables published in 1992 came as a real shock to Queen's. It rated 476 out of the country's top 1,000 schools published in the *Financial Times* list. The school believed that it had to act immediately. But the idea that league tables should control the policy of the school was anathema to Queen's College, founded on F. D. Maurice's belief that education should be for its own sake and not used as an opportunity for 'competitive self-aggrandisement'.

The School is proud of the way it brings out the best in girls who are not necessarily academic high-flyers, but the Council decided that the league tables could not be ignored. Getting into Queen's became harder. The School became more selective. A girl had to have good grades and only if she showed exceptional promise was she likely to be offered a place on poor marks in the entrance exam. In the past Queen's had allowed most girls to sit for external exams whatever their grades, but from then on there was an assessment of every pupil's progress and some, who were not going to make the grade, were asked to leave. Lady Goodhart's view was clear. 'Girls who really can't cope or simply won't work, for whatever reason, should not be at Queen's. They should be in a school that is less demanding and where they might be happier.' She believed that 'tightening up academic achievements at Queen's will, however, never mean that a high place in the league tables becomes an end in itself'.

A change that could have had an effect on the School was the phasing out of the Assisted Places Scheme, a government scheme that paid a proportion of the fees for gifted pupils whose parents could not afford to

The Library.

The computer laboratory.

send them to a fee-paying school. The Assisted Places Scheme benefited hundreds of girls. One of Queen's Assisted Place holders was Vanessa Walters who left in 1995. She wrote a best-selling novel called *Rude Girls* during the long summer holiday after her GCSE examinations, which for a while was on the W. H. Smith best-seller list. She is now on her third novel, continuing a tradition of pupils from all walks of life.

Sophie Thorburn laying a posy on the Memorial Stone of
Bishop Chenevix Trench – a former Dean of Westminster.

CHAPTER NINE

150 YEARS AND A NEW CENTURY

QUEEN'S BEGAN LOOKING FORWARD to its sesquicentennial celebration as early as 1996. The specially convened 'Sesqui' committee had first to decide exactly what the word meant (not everyone on the committee was an academic) and how to make it trip off the tongue. 150 years of Queen's was to be celebrated in the summer of 1998. Was it the sesquicentenary or the sesquicentennial? Just 'Sesqui' would do and the committee, chaired by the Principal with a full-time secretary, first Sarah Witherby and then Janice Lavery (whose daughter was at Queen's), put into action a myriad of decisions arrived at by a committee comprising teachers, a Council member, old girls, and a former Principal, Mrs Fierz.

At times it must have seemed as if 1948, the last big excuse for a celebration, had time-warped the committee back fifty years. Mrs Fierz, who revelled at being back at the school making decisions, of course remembered the centenary with great clarity, and had very firm views on what should happen this time round. Any talk of holding the main church service at St Paul's was 'out of the question'. Fifty years ago it was at the Abbey. Besides, two former Principals of Queen's became Dean of Westminster and Mrs Fierz remembered the girls in a crocodile walking to and from the Abbey every Sunday. Any thought of holding the service at that other place in the City simply had to be put aside.

The Lord Mayor of Westminster and the Dean of Westminster arrive at the Abbey for the Sesqui service.

In planning the service one of the Abbey priests mentioned a bust of F. D. Maurice. No one at the school had heard of it so members of the Sesqui committee were despatched as a search party. It was located on a high ledge in St George's Chapel, alongside a bust of his friend Charles Kingsley, another nineteenth-century luminary, who had also taught at Queen's. Further rummaging in Poets' corner located a bust of the composer William Sterndale Bennett – another teacher from the early days at Queen's. A bouquet of flowers to be placed in front of the busts was then planned for the big day at the Abbey on 26 March 1998.

But to fit everything in, Sesqui events had to start in November 1997, when the girls staged Gilbert and Sullivan's *Princess Ida*. It was a satire on women's education and was inspired by Alfred Tennyson's poem 'The Princess'. That in turn is said to have drawn its inspiration from F. D. Maurice's vision of a college for women. *Queen's News* trumpeted 'What a splendid way to start the Sesqui celebrations. The production was a showcase for Queen's talents. We have come to expect enthusiasm and energy from the annual production, but this time there was something more. It was polished, disciplined and thoroughly professional.' It was also a sellout. Sadly it is not recorded what the founder thought of Gilbert and Sullivan's reworking of Tennyson's 'The Princess': Maurice, it transpires, was not known for his sense of humour!

Remembered as the founder of Queen's, if not the prime mover in the formative days before 1848, Maurice was the subject of John Grigg's Sesqui lecture in November 1997. A distinguished writer and journalist, he was introduced by another eminent biographer and politician, the Rt. Hon. Lord Jenkins of Hillhead. Grigg, some of whose comments were considered in an earlier chapter, surprised the audience by comparing Maurice with Gandhi: 'Maurice resembles Gandhi in the quiet force of his personality, which made him an acknowledged leader among his contemporaries, and, as time went on, among many younger people who were drawn to him. One of the differences between the two men does not, unfortunately favour Maurice: he lacked Gandhi's humour. He was a learned, lovable and inspiring man, but not a funny man. Jokes in his case had to be either unconscious or at his expense.'

Grigg called his lecture 'F. D. Maurice the Reluctant Radical', alluding to his conservative views on socialism which included anathema to trade unions. 'Is it paradoxical to say that Maurice's mind had great insight and subtlety, but was also confused ? Maybe so; but Maurice was a creature of paradox and only a paradox can do justice to him.'

The College filled ten London buses to transport everyone to Westminster Abbey.

Some of the lectures focused on famous old girls. Gertrude Bell, perhaps a little obscure to today's community at Queen's, is remembered by a plaster bust in the main corridor – its brass plaque so highly polished that it will soon be hard to read. Her remarkable life was outlined in a lecture entitled 'Gertrude Bell: Empire Builder or Conservationist' by Sir Stephen Egerton who served as Oriental Secretary in Baghdad in the 1960s. He told the audience that forty years before he arrived, Gertrude Bell had held the same post, along with the job of Curator of Antiquities at the archaeological museum in Baghdad. A descendant of hers, Dr William Plowden, Associate Director of Atlantic Fellowships, chaired the event and introduced the speaker who began by describing Gertrude Bell's writing that was inspired by her travels just after the turn of the century. 'Between 1905 and 1914 there were six major journeys. Starting from Jerusalem, where she spent several months studying Arabic she "did" the Levant and Syria, gradually getting into more and more dangerous terrain, always on the lookout for another ancient archaeological site.

Left to right: Mrs Marie Patterson, Chairman of the Council, Lady Goodhart and Madeleine McGowan, Senior Student on the day of the Sesqui service.

'To make Ottoman officials take her seriously, and to reduce the chances of opportunistic attacks, she travelled heavy, as a great lady, with servants and a baggage train. After the Levant and Syria she turned to Mesopotamia, travelling down the Euphrates and incidentally discovering the lost Sassanian fortress, Ukhaidir, Southwest of Karbala, in 1909.'

At times she feared for her life but her camel train, with its evening dresses, silver cutlery and starched tablecloths and napkins, came to rest at the outbreak of the Great War. Recognizing Gertrude's experience and skills in the Middle East the British government recruited her for intelligence work in Cairo.

Still on the pay-roll of HMG in 1922, she was a friend and adviser to the newly minted royal family of Iraq and honorary curator of the museum in Baghdad, at a time when Iraq was in danger of losing much of its ancient past to 'archaeologists' from Europe and America. 'Gertrude spent a lot of each year visiting sites as excavations progressed, to ensure that everything was above board, and to preside on site over how the archaeological finds should be distributed (foreign expeditions could claim fifty per cent of the finds).

'So much travelling made her progressively more exhausted; she found it difficult to eat much after long days and to sleep. But the gain to the Iraq Museum of her personal attention, at a time when foreign excavation was at its height, remains incalculable.'

Perhaps the lonely bust in the corridor may cause a future young

139

archaeologist to pause and reflect on that remarkable life. Gertrude Bell's collection of antiquities still survives, and the library of the British School of Archaeology in Baghdad is largely intact.

Other lectures in the series were given by Janet Howarth of St Hilda's College, Oxford, on the importance of Queen's in women's education. She called her lecture 'Maybe Wildest Dreams are but the Preludes of the Truth'. In the chair to introduce the speaker was a former minister of education, the Rt. Hon Gillian Shephard. Dr Johanna Geyer-Kordesch, director of the Wellcome Institute for the History of Medicine, University of Glasgow, lectured on Queen's contribution to opening up science to women. She called her lecture, which was chaired by Dr Jane Somerville of the Royal Brompton Hospital, 'Sophia Jex-Blake – Crusader against Prejudice'.

But the lecture that drew the largest audience, including more Queen's girls that any other, was about Katherine Mansfield. The lecture, given by Mansfield's biographer Claire Tomalin, and introduced by Professor Hermione Lee of the University of York, was oversubscribed and a video link had to be set up in the gym for the overflow. Mansfield's name is always trotted out when the School tries to impress, and previous books about her have concentrated on her inspiration from 'leaping fires' at Queen's in her formative years, avoiding the gritty dark side of her past.

Many devotees of Mansfield must have stirred uncomfortably as Claire Tomalin's warts-and-all approach unfolded from the platform. Working with new material, some of which we looked at in a previous chapter, Claire revealed an emotional and sex life that was as tortured and lurid as anything that Hollywood might have manufactured.

The Sesqui committee warmly endorsed an idea from one of the teaching staff that there should be a Victorian day during which everyone at Queen's should ape the appearance and behaviour of girls and teachers 100 years ago. Queen's did a deal with a fancy dress hire company to which the girls sent their measurements, and ten pounds, through the post. They had to provide their own shoes, and to the relief of the organizers, most of them resisted the easy option of familiar multi-coloured trainers. A search of the basement revealed a cache of old nibs and pens; fifteen upright desks were acquired, and Room A was transformed into a genuine-looking schoolroom of the end of the century.

When the girls arrived they were let in by Matthew, the caretaker (not just Matt on that occasion), dressed as the porter who was always on duty at the front door in the nineteenth century. Inside, the main corridor was

Dr Eleanor Relle, Head of English, delivering a lecture to the sixth form in the Library on Victorian Day, under the gaze of F. D. Maurice.

full of teachers in period dress led by Lady Goodhart wearing a voluminous purple number which was set off by an enormous feathered hat. Jim Hutchinson covered one of his famous luminous ties with a natty cravat. The day began with notices in prayers that were read a century ago; girls attended classes in elocution, mental arithmetic and sewing. Mrs Edlin gave a French lesson from a book that her grandmother used at Queen's which was entitled *French Without Tears*.

At times the Queen's theatre spilled out into Harley Street when Miss Lang and Mrs Harrison took the girls for a constitutional. Demurely they walked in crocodile style and stoutly resisted the temptation to shout back at builders hanging on to scaffolding poles who ribbed them mercilessly. A parlour concert with suitably sentimental songs was put on by the Music department and in the basement a 'Victorian' lunch got under way. Instead of self-service the caterers provided waitresses and a menu from Mrs Beeton's famous household book that included wobbly blancmange. A maths wizard calculated that the cost of the meal worked out at one and eleven pence halfpenny each. The effect of crinolines and genteel service was remarkable. Staff on duty were stunned. The girls all behaved so well, passing things to each other like perfect little ladies instead of creating the usual basement bedlam that characterizes lunch time. Perhaps the arrival of a TV camera induced a certain amount of decorum.

The idea that the doors of Queen's should be opened to the media on the occasion of the Sesqui was carefully debated. Some members thought that it could backfire on the School, that an unsympathetic interviewer could tear the School's reputation to shreds. The view that all publicity is good publicity (especially when the important contribution from state-funded assisted places was about to evaporate) won the vote, and a producer working for the Carlton TV *First Edition* showed interest. The BBC radio programme *Women's Hour* also did a long interview about the school with the Principal. Like flies on the wall the cameras became so familiar that the girls soon forgot about them and people behaved more or less naturally as they were filmed during the school day.

Founder's Day 1998, the centrepiece of the Sesqui celebrations, began with a buffet VIP lunch at Queen's. The guests had also been invited to the Founder's Day service at the Abbey and to get them there a fleet of red double-decker buses was hired. One bus that was carrying the school choir become embroiled in a demonstration in Whitehall and arrived at the great west door with only minutes to spare. They sang superbly well.

The senior student Madeleine McGowan read the founder's prayer for the College and the Reverend Mark Santer, Bishop of Birmingham, opened his remarks about the School with some personal memories. 'We are here to thank God for one hundred and fifty years of Queen's College, London. Is that a short or a long time? 1848 was three years before the Great Exhibition. Albert the Prince consort was still alive. So was the Duke of Wellington. That feels like a long time ago. But let me tell you a story. In 1972 I preached a sermon in a Cambridge college chapel about your founder. The occasion was the centenary of his death. After the service one of the older Fellows of the college came up to me and said, "I don't usually come to chapel but I wanted to hear what you said about Maurice. You see, my father preached at his funeral." That feels like not so long ago.'

After the service the double-deckers drew up outside the Abbey to ferry about 800 guests back to the biggest tea party ever put on at Queen's. Every room of any size clattered with teacups and trays of cucumber sandwiches. Girls and the staff looked after their guests, and fielded questions from octogenarian Old Queen's. Eleanor Relle, Head of English since 1989, had to keep smiling through conversations that centred on the virtues of Miss Holloway (Principal 1932–1940) 'best English teacher that Queen's has ever had – don't get teachers like that these days'. Other conversations elicited that three generations of Queen's girls from the same family were sipping tea together, and that a great-granddaughter would probably follow them into the School. Several descendants of F. D.

The Rt. Hon. Lord Jenkins of Hillhead unveils a plaque, 18 November 1997, as part of the College's sesquicentenary commemorative events.

Maurice attended the party including Jenny Sanders, a member of the governing Council. The day was splendid – a triumph of organization – Celia Goodhart, indeed the whole of Queen's that day, was bursting with joy and pride.

A year after the triumph of the Sesqui celebrations Celia Goodhart retired and the new Principal, Margaret Connell, took up her post in September 1999 and immediately set a record. She is the first Principal of Queen's in 150 years to have come to the job from the headship of another school. Her previous school, More House School in Kensington, London, was often in close contact with Harley Street and indeed More House and Queen's drew their pupils from many of the same prep schools. Moreover, Celia Goodhart and Margaret Connell had become headmistresses at the same time and had worked together as secretary and chairman of the London region of the Girls' Schools Association for two years until Margaret took over the chairman's role from Celia. The two Principals agree that their schools shared the same ideals.

Margaret Connell's career has followed a path that is familiar to many heads. Born in Derbyshire into a family of teachers, she attended St Mary's College in Leeds, and in 1966 went up to Lady Margaret Hall, Oxford, to read Physics. Later, with a postgraduate certificate in education from Leeds University, she taught at Headington School in Oxford for six years and at the North London Collegiate School from 1976 to 1986. She was Deputy Head Mistress at Bromley High School for five years before taking over More House in 1991. During eight years as headmistress she inspired a steady development in the school's academic results, particularly in science and mathematics, but she nurtured its cultural life too, music being her special love.

Seven years on, with a successful inspection behind her at More House, Margaret was looking for another challenge along her copybook career path and she saw Queen's as a school which would have the same vision and energy which had impressed her so much in her years at North London. In her application to become Principal at Queen's she wrote about the pioneering spirit of North London Collegiate and Queen's, explaining that she saw at Queen's the opportunity to lead another exciting school, but one of a size where individual relationships can be preserved and the girls given freedom to develop their personalities to the full.

The first thing that struck her about Queen's was the size of the place. There was much more space behind that eighteenth-century façade than

Margaret Connell, Principal since 1999.

143

she had imagined – and more opportunity to create modern facilities that will serve the School better in the twenty-first century. Each year the number of potential pupils trooping though the door of 43 Harley Street grows larger. Fears that the School might be in trouble when the Assisted Places Scheme was phased out proved to be unfounded and applicants were at an all-time high for the year beginning September 2000.

Parents seem to be less stressed about league tables now and respond well to Margaret Connell's view: 'what Queen's is trying to do is give every girl the opportunity to do as well as she can and better than expected'. Parents, she believes, are happy with that concept. 'The league tables are self-perpetuating. A school's position may change by a dozen or so places but from year to year there are no major shifts.' This, however, is not a return to a *laissez-faire* approach to results. 'Our aim is to raise the proportion of higher grades at GCSE level. We need to raise expectations and structure the curriculum, and the way the girls are taught, to help them do better.' The Principal is on record as saying that: 'the circumstances would have to be truly exceptional for any girl to be asked to leave'.

The selection process is important. Margaret herself sees all the 11-year-olds separately and then with their parents. The girls are asked to bring a piece of work along to the interview – something they have written or made, or perhaps a musical instrument. During the interview the Principal might try to explore a subject raised in the interview by using books from the library or by taking the girl over to the computer terminal on her desk – the first head at Queen's who can surf the internet and communicate with her staff by e-mail – to interrogate a web site somewhere in the world.

A significant proportion of the applicants are from state schools where they might have been taught in classes of thirty or more. They are up against prep school girls who have been prepared for examinations in much smaller classes and Margaret Connell believes that this could make a huge difference in their marks. 'The girl's performance in the written examination is important but at the interview I am looking for that telltale spark in her eye that shows me she wants to learn more.'

Educational history has been made for over a century and a half since the crinolines and chaperones first arrived at the door of number 43 Harley Street. Queen's is a thoroughly modern institution which continues to reflect traditions that were established by its founders in the mid-nineteenth century, and takes its place today among the most successful of the independent girls' schools in the London catchment area. As Celia Goodhart remarked, 'This is a remarkable place with a remarkable history. We are full of contradictions: an Anglican foundation, and we currently embrace those of almost every known religion and none. The plaster mouldings and wrought-iron balustrades embellish eighteenth-century rooms that can contain anything from modernized laboratories for the sciences and computing, to experimental electronic music.'

Margaret Connell, a new Principal for a new millennium, had an insight into the special quality of Queen's when she presided over her first Queen's open day. Before the prospective parents and 11-year-olds arrived for their first glimpse behind the scenes, she called the senior girls together and asked them what they thought was important about Queen's, and what the visitors should be told. The advice was unanimous: 'tell them about the library, and tell them about the staff'. Despite all the advances in technology that will accompany the school into the new millennium, it is still the quality of its teaching staff which preserves the individual character of Queen's: long may it remain so.

Queen's playing fields in the beautiful setting of Regent's Park.

PRINCIPALS OF QUEEN'S COLLEGE

Revd R. Chenevix Trench (Dean of
    Westminster)
1863–1872 Revd A. P. Stanley (Dean
    of Westminster)
1873–1874 Revd J. Llewelyn Davies
    (brother of Emily Davies,
    founder of Girton)
1875–1879 Revd E. Plumptre
1879–1886 Revd J. Llewelyn Davies

1886–1894 Canon R. Elwyn
1895–1898 Revd C. J. Robinson
1898–1903 Revd T. W. Sharpe (a for-
    mer Chief Inspector of
    HMI)
1904–1910 Canon G. C. Bell
1911–1915 Sir Henry Craik (first lay
    Principal)
1915–1918 Revd J. F. Kendall

1919–1931 Mr Joseph Edwards
1932–1940 Miss G. E. Holloway
1940–1942 Miss A. M. Kynaston
    (acting Principal)
1942–1964 Miss A. M. Kynaston
1964–1983 Mrs S. Fierz
1983–1990 Mrs P. J. Fleming
1991–1999 Lady Goodhart
1999–   Margaret Connell

QUEEN'S COLLEGE
AT THE TIME OF THE SESQUICENTENARY

COUNCIL OF QUEEN'S COLLEGE
Mrs M. Patterson CBE BA (London)
    D.Sc. (Hon.) (Salford)
Chairman TUC 1974–5 and 1977;
Member of General Council of the
    TUC 1963–84;
Equal Opportunities Commission
    1975–84;
Council, Office of Banking
    Ombudsman;
Governor of the LSE

His Honour Judge John Byrt QC MA
    (Oxon.)
Judge of the Mayors and City of
    London Court

Mrs J. Campbell CMG MA (Oxon.)
Mistress of Girton College, Cambridge
    and OQ

Lady Chorley
Wife of recent Chairman of the
    National Trust

Bernard Clow Esq FCA
Partner, KPMG and former parent

Mrs D. Davis (*née* Wolfson) BA
    (Manchester)
Solicitor and journalist and OQ

Lady Hopkins AA Dipl. Hon. FAIA
    Hon. FRIAS
Architect; Partner, Michael Hopkins &
    Partners and former parent

Mrs J. Jones MA (Brunel) B.Sc.
    (Econ.) (Wales)
Director of Social Services,
    Westminster City Council and cur-
    rent parent

Miss C. Kenyon Jones MA (Oxon.)
Director of PR, King's College London

Peter Lewis Esq MA (Oxon.)
Former Chairman of John Lewis PLC
    and former parent

Mrs V. Potter BA (London)
Former member of staff

Mrs J. Pulay MA (Oxon.)
Executive Director, Morgan Stanley &
    Co.

Mrs C. Rumboll (*née* Pilkington)
Cert. Ed. (Cambridge) Dip.Soc.
    (London)
President, Old Queen's Society;
Chairman, Hugh Pilkington Charitable
    Trust;
Member of the Chancellor's Court of
    Benefactors, Oxford University

Mrs J. Sanders
Great-greatgranddaughter of the
    founder of Queen's, F. D. Maurice

David Summerscale Esq MA (Cantab.)
Head Master, Westminster School

Dr J. Somerville (*née* Platnauer) MD
    FRCP FACC
Consultant Physician, Royal Brompton
    and National Heart Hospital and
    OQ

Lady Trethowan JP
Widow of former Director-General,
    BBC

Desmond Wilcox Esq
Journalist and broadcaster and current
    parent

PATRON
HM the Queen Mother

VISITOR
The Lord Bishop of London

PRINCIPAL
The Lady Goodhart,
MA (Oxon.), Honorary Fellow of St
    Hilda's College, Oxford

SENIOR MANAGEMENT TEAM
Senior Tutor: J. S. Hutchinson MA,
    M.Sc.
Deputy Senior Tutor: Mrs Y. Brett BA,
    M.Phil.
Senior Mistress: Mrs L. Foord MA
Director of Studies: D. S. Angadi MA
University and Library Tutor: Mrs E.
    Relle MA, Ph.D.
Head of Science: Mrs J. Scott B.Sc.
Bursar and Secretary to the Council:
    Mrs E. C. Chesswas BA
Timetabling: Mrs J. K. Jackson B.Sc.
Examinations Tutor: J. P. Gray MA,
    Ph.D.

LECTURERS AND TEACHERS
IN COLLEGE AND SCHOOL
Full Time
D. S. Angadi MA (Cantab.)
    History
Mrs S. C. Atkins BA (Oxon.)
    Classics/Careers
Mrs S. M. Baker BA (Philadelphia),
    M.Sc. (London)
    Chemistry/Physics
T. S. Bhambra B.Sc. (North London),
    M.Sc. (London), AFIMA, FRAS
    I.T./Mathematics
Mrs Y. Brett BA, M.Phil. (London)
    French

LECTURERS AND TEACHERS (*continued*)

Mrs C. Briscoe BA (London)
English/Theatre Studies/Drama
Miss K. Costar B.Sc. (Massey, New Zealand)
Mathematics
Mrs S. Deans MA (Oxon.), FCA
Geography
J. T. Donovan B.Sc. (London)
Mathematics
Miss C. Drower BA (Kingston)
Art
Mrs B. R. Edlin MA (Dublin.)
German/French
Miss F. Elderkin B.Sc. (Exeter)
Biology
Mrs L. Foord MA (St Andrews), MA (London)
French/Japanese
Miss G. Foschi BA (London)
Italian/Spanish
J. P. Gray Art MA (Oxon.), Ph.D. (London)
History of Art/Art
Mrs S. Harrison MA (Oxon.)
Classics
J. S. Hutchinson BA, MA (London), M.Sc. (Kingston)
Classics
Mrs J. K. Jackson B.Sc. (London)
Mathematics
Mrs M. Kateck BA (McGill), MA (London)
History
Miss S. J. Kittle B.Sc. (Salford)
Physics
Miss A. Lang BA (Oxon.)
Classics
Miss U. J. M. Lynam BA (Oxon.)
Italian/French
Miss C. Mackenzie Smith BA (Oxon.)
Spanish/German/French
Miss R. Martinez BA (Kent), MA (Birmingham)
Art/History of Art/Junior Mistress
Miss T. Millar B.Ed. (Durham)
P.E./School Mistress
Mrs E. Murray B.Sc. (Wales)
Biology/Science
Mrs N. Peace BA (St Petersburg)
Russian/French
Mrs E. Relle MA, Ph.D. (Cantab.)
English/Theatre Studies
J. R. Rose BA (Kingston)
Music
Mrs J. Scott B.Sc. (London)
Chemistry/Science

Mrs H. Sperling BA (London), FRGS
Geography/R.S.
Miss L. Walker BA (Oxon.)
English/Drama
Mrs A. Wells B.Sc. (Canterbury)
Mathematics/Economics/P.E.
Mrs V. Weston B.Sc. (UEA), B.Th. (Oxon.)
Religious Studies
Miss H. Wilder B.Sc. (London)
Mathematics
Miss E. D. M. Woodhouse BA (Oxon.)
English/Drama

Part Time
E. D. Bird BA (Wimbledon)
IT
Miss N. Daines
Dance
J. D. Ferrar BA (Cantab.)
English/Drama
Miss L. Harris BA
Fencing
Mrs C. M. Huckin B.Ed. (Sussex)
Physical Education
Miss M. Kelly BA (York)
Music
Miss C. Lax LRAM, LTCL
Director of Music (Administration)
W. G. Munro BA (Cantab.)
Information Technology
Mrs L. Penny BA (Oxon.)
Classics
C. A. F. Stephens BA (Oxon.)
Government/Politics
Mrs S. Stopford AB (Radcliffe), BA (Cantab.)
English
Mrs C. E. Walker BA (Cantab.)
Religious Studies

MUSIC DEPARTMENT
Miss S. Blair GRSM, LRAM
Piano
A. Caldon Dip. RAM
Brass
Mrs S. Hambleton-Smith LRAM
Guitar
Miss M. Kelly BA (York)
Violin
Miss C. Lax LRAM, LTCL
Principal Accompanist/Piano/Singing
W. Leigh Knight AGSM
Singing
Miss J. Phillips Dip. RCM
Cello
P. Robinson FTCL, LLCM

Woodwind/Theory
Miss I. Tasic B.Mus.
Harp
Miss C. de Sybel BA (Cantab.)
Piano/Theory
A. Timperley LTCL
Clarinet/Saxophone

BURSAR
Mrs E. C. Chesswas BA (O.U.)
Miss A. Ayo LLB(London)
Assistant (Part Time)

COLLEGE LIBRARIAN AND ARCHIVIST
Mrs J. Fitz Gerald MA (Cantab.)

COLLEGE SECRETARY
Mrs M. I. Brunyate BA, MA (London)
Miss M. Paterson BA (Oxon.)
Assistant (Part Time)

FINANCE STAFF
Mrs L. Thompson
Finance Officer
W. Leigh Knight AGSM
(Part Time) Assistant Finance Officer

REGISTRAR
Mrs J. M. L. Pearce

SCHOOL NURSE
Miss S. P. Hutchison BA (Victoria, New Zealand)

SESQUICENTENNIAL SECRETARY
Mrs J. M. Lavery
Miss C. Tapper BA (Oxon.)
Assistant

SUPPORT STAFF
K. P. Anderson OND
Senior Laboratory Technician
Mrs L. Austin HNC
Laboratory Technician
M. Kevin
Caretaker/Maintenance
M. J. Hutchinson BA (London)
IT Network Manager
J. D. Ferrar BA (Cantab.)
Media Resources Officer/Language Laboratory Technician

SESQUICENTENARY EVENTS

5–8 November 1997
Princess Ida
by Gilbert & Sullivan
Written in 1884 as a satire on Queen's and the movement for women's education

18 November 1997
Public Lecture
'F. D. Maurice – Reluctant Radical'
Christian Socialist and Founder of Queen's College
Given by John Grigg, Historian and Journalist
Chaired by the Rt. Hon. Lord Jenkins of Hillhead OM, Chancellor of the University of Oxford

27 January 1998
'Katherine Mansfield – The Wild Colonial Girl'
Writer and former pupil of Queen's College
Given by Claire Tomalin, journalist and writer; author of *Katherine Mansfield: A Secret Life*
Chaired by Professor Hermione Lee FRSL, Professor of English Literature, University of York

26 March 1998
Westminster Abbey
Founder's Day Service
Preacher
The Rt. Revd Mark Santer, Bishop of Birmingham
Tea at Queen's College

27 April 1998
'Gertrude Bell – Empire Builder or Conservationist?'
Archaeologist, journalist and former pupil of Queen's College
Given by Sir Stephen Egerton KCMG, Vice-President, the British School of Archaeology in Iraq; formerly Ambassador to Italy, Albania, Saudi Arabia and Iraq
Chaired by Dr William Plowden, great-nephew of Gertrude Bell; Associate Director, Atlantic Fellowships

1 May 1998
Victorian Day
On the anniversary of the opening of the College, a re-creation by staff and pupils of a Victorian schoolday
Half-day holiday

22 June 1998
'Sophia Jex-Blake – Crusader against Prejudice'
The pioneer woman doctor, educational campaigner and former pupil of Queen's College
Given by Dr Johanna Geyer-Kordesch MA Ph.D. Med.habil, Director of the Wellcome Unit for the History of Medicine, University of Glasgow
Chaired by Dr Jane Somerville MD FRCP FACC FESC, Consultant Physician for Congenital Heart Diseases, Director of Grown-Up Congenital Heart Unit, the Royal Brompton Hospital

2 July 1998
Annual Gathering
The Annual Report to the Visitor,
The Rt. Revd & Rt. Hon. Richard Chartres, the Lord Bishop of London
Tea
Concert
at St Peter's, Vere Street, W1
Drinks Party
for all current parents and 1998 Senior College leavers

7 July 1998
Grand Gathering
Old Queen's Summer Party: The Grand Reunion

22 September 1998
Public Lecture
'"Maybe wildest dreams are but the needful preludes of the truth": The Place of Queen's College in the History of Women's Education'
Given by Mrs Janet Howarth MA, Fellow and Tutor in History, St Hilda's College, Oxford
Chaired by the Rt. Hon. Gillian Shephard MP, Shadow Leader of the House of Commons

DISTINGUISHED OLD QUEENS

Nineteenth Century

DOROTHEA BEALE (1848–55), *founder of Cheltenham Ladies' College and St Hilda's College, Oxford*

FRANCES MARY BUSS (1848), *founder of North London Collegiate School*

FRANCES DOVE (1860–2), *founder of Wycombe Abbey and second head-mistress of St Leonard's School and St Andrew's*

SOPHIA JEX-BLAKE (1858–61), *co-founder of the London School of Medicine*

GERTRUDE BELL (1884–6), *diplomat, archaeologist and cartologist*

Twentieth Century

CICELY COURTNEIDGE (1905–6), *actress*

PENELOPE GILLIATT (1942–7), *journalist and writer*

KATHLEEN HALTON TYNAN (1951–5), *journalist*

SALLY ANN HOWES (1937–8), *actress*

KATHLEEN KENNEDY (1938), *Marchioness of Hartington, sister of John F. Kennedy*

Jacqueline Du Pré

KATHERINE MANSFIELD (1903–6), *author*

CHRISTINA ONASSIS (1967–8)

JACQUELINE DU PRÉ (1959), *'cellist*

DIANA BARNATO WALKER (1928–34), *pilot and author*

Contemporary

LESLEY ABDELA (1962), *feature writer, author and broadcaster*

EMMA ANDERSON (1982–4), *recording artist (Lush)*

HARRIET ANSTRUTHER (1978–85), *textile designer*

Pop group 'Lush', with members Miki Berenyi (second left) and Emma Anderson (far right).

MIKI BERENYI (1980–5), *recording artist (Lush)*

SELINA BLOW (1982–3), *fashion designer*

DIANA BRAHAMS (1959–61), *legal practitioner and freelance writer*

TANIA BRYER (1973–80), *broadcaster*

JULIET CAMPBELL (1951–3), *Mistress of Girton College, Cambridge*

Emma Freud

HARRIET CASS (1962–70), *broadcaster*

DAME ELIZABETH CHESTERTON DBE (1932), *architect*

SUSANNAH CONSTANTINE (1978), *journalist*

LISA FREEDMAN (1967–73), *journalist*

LADY KAREN FISHER (1968–70), *farmer*

EMMA FREUD (1973–80), *broadcaster*

POLLY GHAZI (1978–81), *journalist and writer*

BELINDA GILES (1968–75), *independent television producer*

DAISY GOODWIN (1972–7), *BBC television producer*

JOY HANCOCK (1963–5), *Head, Bromley High School*

LADY HENDERSON (1927–35), *designer and writer*

DAME ROSALINDE HURLEY DBE (1948–50), *Professor of Microbiology, University of London, at Institute of Obstetrics and Gynaecology (Royal Postgraduate Medical School), 1975–95*

TAMARA INGRAM (1972–9), *CEO Saatchi & Saatchi*

Professor Hermione Lee.

CAROLINE LEE JOHNSON (1980–2),
actress

PROFESSOR HERMIONE LEE (1963–5),
*biographer and Goldsmith Professor of
English Literature, Oxford*

PROFESSOR ALBINIA DE LA MARE
OBE (1947–56), *Professor of
Palaeography, King's College London*

DEBORAH MOGGACH (1959–62),
writer and novelist

MARGARET MORRIS (1972–4), *dancer*

DAME ALISON MUNRO DBE
(1924–5), *High Mistress, St Paul's
Girls' School 1964–74*

Claudia Rosencrantz.

DAME SIMONE PRENDERGAST DBE JP
DL (1939–40)

BELLA POLLEN (1977),
fashion designer and writer

PROFESSOR GRISELDA POLLOCK
(1964–6), *art historian*

JANE PROCTER (1970–2), *editor of*
Tatler

JOYCE ROSE CBE JP DL (1946–50),
ex-chairman, Magistrates' Association

CLAUDIA ROSENCRANTZ (1975–9),
ITV Controller of Entertainment

BERNICE SANDELSON (1947–55),
gallery owner

DR ANN SAUNDERS (1946–8),
independent historian and lecturer

GILLIAN SHEEN (1945–7),
Olympic fencing gold medallist

EMMA SOAMES (1965–7), *journalist*

Barbara Thompson.

LADY SOAMES [MARY CHURCHILL]
(1940), *Chairman Royal National
Theatre Board*

DR JANE SOMERVILLE (1944–50),
*Consultant, The Royal Brompton and
National Heart Hospital*

Susannah Wise.

ELIZABETH STUART-SMITH (1978–80),
shoe designer

SUE SUMMERS (1962–9), *journalist*

ROSEMARY TIBBER (1943–7), *author*

BARBARA THOMPSON MBE
(1955–62), *musician*

SOPHIE WARD (1976–83), *actress*

SUSANNAH WISE (1984–91), *actress*

ANNA WINTOUR (1960–3), *editor of*
American Vogue

INDEX

Numbers <u>underlined</u> refer to a colour facing page

PICTURE ACKNOWLEDGEMENTS

The Cheltenham Ladies' College 19 (both); Emma Freud 149; Girton College 66 (bottom), 67 (top); Hulton Getty Picture Collection 11 (bottom), 51, 75, 76 (bottom), 85, 94, 95 (top), 107, 149 (bottom left); Imperial War Museum 86; Hermione Lee 150 (© Jane Brown); 'Lush' 149 (photo by Andrew Catlin); Mary Evans 14, 16, 18, 20 (both), 21, 24, 29, 30, 31, 65; National Portrait Gallery 13 (bottom), 22, 32, 41 (right), 45 (all), 51, 60 (bottom); National Trust Photographic Library 48 (painting by John Hammond); North London Collegiate School 63; Queen Mary & Westfield College 44; Claudia Rosencrantz 150; The Royal Archives © Her Majesty Queen Elizabeth II 71 (bottom), 76 (top); Scottish National Portrait Gallery 23 (painting by Thomas Philips); Barbara Thompson 150 (photo by David Redfern); V&A Picture Library 80; Wellcome Library, London 64; Westminster City Archives 12 (both), 13 (top); Susannah Wise 150.

The quote which appears on page 71–2 is reproduced by kind permission of Her Majesty The Queen.